The political phenomenon known as the 'Springtime of the Nations' swept through Europe in 1848, toppling thrones, forcing old autocratic regimes to grant constitutions to the people and bringing street fighting and large scale campaigns to cities and states across the continent. What is not generally known is that a precursor to these events had already taken place in the centre of Europe in the Alpine valleys of the collection of independent states known collectively as Switzerland. In November 1847, twelve of the Swiss cantons went to war with seven other cantons over the future of the country. The campaign lasted just three weeks, with only a few hundred casualties and ended with the establishment of the modern Swiss state we have today. If it had not ended so quickly it is likely that France, Austria and Prussia would have become involved, which would have led to a European-wide war.

This book is unique in that it concentrates on the military aspects of this episode in history. As well as an outline of the campaign itself, it covers the strengths and organisation of each canton; in 1847 each was a separate state with its own army. Included are chapters on the uniforms of the cantons' armies, their battle flags, weapons and distinguishing badges. The major battle of the war, at Gislikon (modern Gisikon), a small village with a strategic river crossing, just north of the city of Luzern, is treated in detail. As well as the general picture, individual soldiers' stories illustrate the combat techniques of the period.

Biographies are given of some of the leading figures from both sides of the conflict, which demonstrate the European dimension. Many served in French, Dutch and Neapolitan armies before taking appointments in the Swiss canton armies.

To compliment the text the book is well illustrated with a mixture of contemporary pictures, in colour and black and white, and also specially produced colour plates of Swiss canton uniforms and flags. So that the reader can follow the campaign, maps from official Swiss sources are included. Orders of battle for all the cantons and detailed orders of battle for the main action at Gisikon are also provided.

I0868958

Ralph Weaver has made a life-long study of military history, particularly of Europe in the 19th Century. He began his military career with the Sealed Knot before giving up the sword for the pen. He has been the editor of the journal of the Continental Wars Society for the past twenty-five years and has written and illustrated books and magazine articles on military history. He trained as a land surveyor in the Civil Service and has used his map-making skills in battlefield walking and table top wargaming. He has been collecting books, pictures, photographs and reference material on uniforms with a view to writing a definitive history on the subject. As well as conducting research on military topics, his latest interests include cooking and looking after grandchildren.

THREE WEEKS IN NOVEMBER

A MILITARY HISTORY OF THE SWISS CIVIL WAR OF 1847

Ralph Weaver

Helion & Company Ltd

Helion & Company Limited
Unit 8 Amherst Business Centre
Budbrooke Road
Warwick
CV34 5WE
England
Tel. 01926 499619
Email: info@helion.co.uk
Website: www.helion.co.uk
X (formerly Twitter): @Helionbooks
Facebook: @HelionBooks
Visit our blog at https://helionbooks.wordpress.com/

Published by Helion & Company 2012. This paperback edition 2025
Designed and typeset by Farr out Publications, Wokingham, Berkshire
Cover designed by Paul Hewitt, Battlefield Design (www.battlefield-design.co.uk)

ISBN 978-1-804518-49-6

British Library Cataloguing-in-Publication Data.
A catalogue record for this book is available from the British Library.

For details of other military history titles published by Helion & Company Limited, contact the above address, or visit our website: http://www.helion.co.uk

We always welcome receiving book proposals from prospective authors.

Contents

List of Illustrations

Images in colour section

List of Maps

Introduction

This book covers a conflict little known in the English-speaking world, the civil war in Switzerland, which lasted for just three weeks in November 1847. Indeed, it is hardly mentioned in many Swiss histories, sometimes meriting only a paragraph or two. The build up to the outbreak of military action had begun much earlier, as a result of the French Revolution, which had spilled over into the Alpine towns, forests and meadows. It really was an age-old question, who are the rulers and who the ruled? The old aristocracy did not let go without a fight, at first diplomatically and finally by force of arms. It seems strange to talk about aristocrats in a land made up of republics, but the old ruling families were long-lived, generation after generation providing the rulers of many of the Swiss cantons.

The following text uses the German names of the cantons for consistency, but where some are better known to English speakers by their French names I have used that name.

German	French
Uri	Uri
Schwyz	Schwyz
Nidwalden	Nidwald
Obwalden	Obwald
Luzern	Lucerne
Zurich	Zurich
Glarus	Glaris
Zug	Zoug
Bern	Berne
Freiburg	Fribourg
Solothurn	Soleure
Basel Stadt	Bale-Ville
Basel Land	Bale-Campagne
Schaffhausen	Schaffhouse
Appenzell[1]	Appenzell
St Gallen	Saint-Gall
Graubunden	Grisons
Aargau	Argovie
Thurgau	Thurgovie
Tessin	Ticino (in Italian)
Waadt	Vaud
Wallis	Valais
Neuenburg	Neuchatel
Genf	Geneva

1 Appenzell was made up of two half cantons, Appenzell (Inner) and Appenzell (Outer).

The canton name was often taken from the chief town, which name was sometimes given to one of the many lakes within the Alpine region. Thus the city of Luzern, the capital of canton Luzern, stood on the east bank of Lake Luzern. In canton Zurich, likewise, the town of Zurich stood at the head of the Lake of Zurich, similarly with Zug.

As the scene for a military campaign, Switzerland was most unsuitable, high mountain ridges separated by many rivers and lakes filling the depressions left over from the last ice age. The main roads followed the river valleys, twisting back and forth through the natural features and climbing over mountain passes where there was no other route. The time taken to travel between locations could not be measured in distance 'as the crow flies', but by the time taken to negotiate the route. In the history of Switzerland invaders had found to their cost that many roads concealed ambushes and that the defenders of their mountain homes could come and slip away without being seen.

The languages used by the Swiss were, and still are, German, French, Italian and a local tongue, a dialect of German. In the list of references at the end of this work most early sources are in German with some published in both German and French versions. Modern works tend to have bilingual texts. Surprisingly, some good, almost contemporary, English accounts of the war appear not in works of history, but in pocket books intended for English tourists. As with most history it tends to be written by the victors, with obvious bias towards the Confederate point of view. English texts also favour the Confederates as they were seen to be espousing a more 'liberal' viewpoint which would appeal to the travelling English public. Conversely, books written by former Sonderbund officers and politicians (often the same people) would try to justify their own position. Language could be an issue among the Swiss, General Dufour was a native French speaker from Geneva, who led an army speaking French, German and Italian.

I have shown, in the various orders of battle, numbers of men in each company, battalion, brigade and division. Sometimes the figures do not appear to add up, or contradict another list; this is because the sources do not agree and themselves show contradictions and inconsistencies. Overall they do give a fairly good picture of the numbers of troops raised by each side in the conflict, and even though the actual fighting did not last long, original musters were only good for the day they were taken. A good example of a reason for the discrepancies in numbers is in the casualty roll. The small numbers of killed and wounded of the Sonderbund armies were gathered by the commanding officer of the Confederation army, General Dufour, and published in the official records. They were possibly kept deliberately low to minimise any animosity and to smooth the process of reconciliation. Other sources (a history of the Luzern forces) give a much higher number of Sonderbund casualties. Some of the men included in the casualty lists did not die on the battlefield, but succumbed later to their wounds, either in a hospital, or back in their home village. There was also a problem with keeping records of Landsturm (Home Guard) companies whose organisation was less rigid than the regular units.

The two sides of the conflict were: firstly, the group of cantons who set up their own separate military alliance, the German word being 'Sonderbund'; secondly, the majority of cantons who were part of the original Confederation founded in 1815. I have tried to avoid using the term 'Federal' for this group, as strictly speaking, the Federal Swiss state only emerged in 1848. However, the Swiss themselves used this term for several official positions, such as the officers of the regular army – the small group of full time officers who were the 'General Staff' and were styled 'Federal Colonel' etc.

1

The Republic in the Mountains

As Europe emerged from the Middle Ages, emperors, kings, princes and bishops ruled the new political states that made up the map. In the centre of the continent, hidden among the forests and peaks of the Alpine mountain range a group of small communities met together to form an alliance of independent states. These corners of land, or cantons, became the origin of the country now known as Switzerland.

They had to fight most of their neighbours to preserve their independence, earning a reputation for military prowess on a level with English and Welsh longbowmen. Over the years other small communities joined the confederation, who although varied in language and religion, all espoused a republican form of government. By the middle years of the 19th Century, the Swiss Confederation consisted of twenty-two cantons, each having one vote in the Confederation parliament (the Diet). The cantons were unequal in wealth and population, Bern having about 430,000 inhabitants, Zurich about 250,000, while Uri had only 15,000. Three of the cantons, Basel, Appenzell and Unterwalden, were divided into two half-cantons, each half having a similar independent status to the full cantons. The two sections of Basel ('Stadt', the town and 'Land', the country) and Appenzell (Inner and Outer) differed from each other and were almost always politically opposed, so that their votes in the Diet tended to cancel each other out. The population of the whole Confederation was about 2.4 million in 1847, with about 900,000 following the Catholic faith.

Contemporary Swiss infantry and cavalry. (Author's collection)

2

The Sonderbund

The early years of the 19th Century were a furious mix of political opinions across Europe and the Swiss were not left untouched. The French Revolution had led to a rise of extreme views, while Napoleon's defeat encouraged the re-establishment of the old aristocratic systems in many countries. In Switzerland, across a number of cantons, a Radical Party was established which sought to modernise the Swiss government by bringing the country into a more Federal union. Its power was mainly centred in the Protestant and urban cantons. Some of its policies were overtly anti-Catholic, such as the dissolution of the many convents and monasteries and selling the land to local people.

Feelings ran very high, especially against the Catholic authorities in Luzern. In 1845 a large group of militants from canton Zurich formed a volunteer armed force, the 'Freicorps' and invaded Luzern territory. They were routed in a bloody fight, with many killed and more taken prisoner. This, if anything, strengthened the resolve of the Sonderbund to resist outside pressure.

The Sonderbund has often been portrayed as a rival Swiss federation composed of the mainly Catholic cantons, with the presence of the Jesuits as the major factor in causing the split. As ever, this is a great over-simplification of the situation. The proposed expulsion of the Jesuits by the majority cantons did indeed become the immediate cause of the war, but this was only the final act in a series of conflicts between the majority of the cantons and the seven who formed the official separate league (as the Sonderbund was called). What was really at stake was the form of government each canton wanted to have.

Siegwart Müller, leader of the Sonderbund. (Author's collection)

After 1815 the general political opinion within the majority of cantons was for a greater democratic form of government and the idea grew that a more centralised Federal state would better serve the whole country. However, those cantons with a Catholic majority also tended to have an aristocratic form of government, whose rulers looked upon the idea of a federal state as an attack on their privileges.

In 1841 the majority in the Confederation council voted to take action against the Catholic church by ordering the closure of monasteries and convents in the canton Aargau and the seizure of their properties. As a provocative act against the majority, the aristocratic cantons set up their separate league and invited the Jesuits into their cantons to run the education system. The Jesuits' avowed aim was to restore the Catholic faith to Switzerland at the expense of Protestantism. The aristocratic parties saw this as a guarantee of their privileges, while the cantons of the Confederation were fearful of foreign (that is, Papal) interference in their country.

While the Jesuits were happy to take over the education system of the Sonderbund states, it is not clear whether they or the canton governments held the real power. The Jesuit priests had a strong influence among the rural populations, but less so in the towns; indeed, many townspeople were not in favour of their own leaders, which would lead to disastrous consequences when it came to military action. It seems clear that the various Sonderbund leaders, particularly in Freiburg and Luzern, were using the Jesuit influence for their own purposes. Was the future of Switzerland to lie with the Sonderbund idea of a loose collection of sovereign states, or a single state on a Federal model? In 1847 each canton had its own flag, its own currency, weights and measures, trade tariffs, postage stamps and other laws that inhibited co-operation. The Sonderbund wished to see this continue, while the Confederation pressed for the Federal solution.

Parade of Sonderbund troops in Freiburg. (*Illustrated London News*)

General Johan Ulrich von Salis-Soglio, commander of the Sonderbund's forces. (Author's collection)

In the summer of 1847, Luzern and its fellow cantons prepared for war openly. A committee of war was established, with representatives from the seven cantons. Large stocks of arms and ammunition were gathered from home and abroad. Other preparations included the building of fortifications and strongpoints around the frontiers and at strategic places within the cantons, especially protecting the cities of Freiburg and Luzern.

The Sonderbund leaders prepared themselves for war against the Confederation. They believed that they would be able to break the rule of the liberal governments and even partition some of the cantons, notably Aargau, and Bern. With their victory the Jesuits were to be allowed to establish themselves throughout the Swiss territories. They relied on the strength of their own forces and the help of the French and Austrians and what they perceived as division and lack of purpose among the other cantons. They convinced themselves of their own people's fanatic devotion to the cause, sadly misplaced, as events were to prove.

In early July 1847 the Confederation Diet met in the city of Bern. It proclaimed a number of decrees against the Sonderbund and the tragic consequences for Switzerland if allowed to continue. Luzern and its six colleagues protested, until on 20 July a decree was passed by 12 and two half votes against seven that the Sonderbund was dissolved. If they did not obey, the Confederation authorised military action to carry out the decree.

The Swiss Federal Treaty of 1815 had forbidden the setting up of separate alliances and the Confederate council declared the Sonderbund to be dissolved. Commissioners were sent to the leaders of the Sonderbund cantons to persuade them to disband peacefully, but without success. In October 1847 the Confederation ordered that the army be mobilised to carry out the order by force.

François Philippe de Maillardoz, commander of the Freiburg Division, Sonderbund army. (Author's collection)

The leader of the Luzern government, and *de facto* head of the Sonderbund, Constantin Siegwart-Müller, had already accepted that military action was inevitable and in early 1847 sought to establish an army to defend the beleaguered cantons. Money and arms were procured from outside the Swiss boundaries. The French government of King Louis Philippe saw that help to the Sonderbund would appease France's own strong Catholic minority and he needed all the friends he could get to support his crumbling throne. Thousands of muskets were smuggled across the French frontier, through Neuenburg and into Freiburg. Austria, always seeing itself as the champion of the Catholic faith, sent a large sum of money that filled the treasury of Luzern, together with a present of 3,000 muskets. At one point it seemed that Austria might also send troops to help the Sonderbund, but it was distracted by troubles in Hungary and Italy.

At first the Pole, Chlapowsky, was considered as commander of the army, and even the name of the Austrian nobleman Friedrich von Schwarzenberg was mentioned, before the Sonderbund council insisted on a Swiss citizen. An experienced officer, a former general in the Neapolitan service, Ludwig von Sonnenberg, and Colonel Philippe de Maillardoz, a former commander of the Swiss troops in French service, were proposed, but the choice eventually fell on Wilhelm von Kalbermatten, commander of the Sonderbund troops in canton Wallis. He preferred to defend his home canton so turned down the appointment. The man eventually given command was Colonel Jean-Ulrich de Salis-Soglio. He had to organise the canton forces into an army and in September and October 1847 asked the various assemblies to authorise a general conscription.

3

The Swiss Canton Armies in 1847

The first truly 'Swiss' army, in the modern sense of the word, was created in 1798 by Napoleon after he had defeated the confederation of Swiss cantons and set up the Helvetian Republic in its place. The new republic had to supply the French with 18,000 men organised into six regiments (or Demi-Brigades as they were termed), each of three battalions. In 1804 Napoleon, now French emperor, had no need of republics and restored a Swiss confederation of semi-autonomous cantons with himself as protector. The new state reorganised its army into four regiments, each of four battalions. The name Switzerland first came into use at this time. In 1815 the Congress of Vienna tried to undo much of Napoleon's heritage and Switzerland reverted to a confederated state of independent cantons. Foreign policy and a national army were reserved to a Diet or council made up of representatives from each canton.

The army, reconstituted in 1817, was not a national force, but consisted of contributions from each canton depending on its population. Every male citizen was obliged to defend the state when called upon, with uniform, arms and equipment supplied by the local community. This not only saved the state vast sums of money as it did not have to support a standing army which proved so ruinous for other European countries, but meant that it could call out a very large army with only a few days notice.

Training for the army usually consisted of an annual camp where the battalions had two weeks' concentrated drill and exercises. By 1847 hardly any of the rank and file had any first hand experience of combat, although some of the senior officers had either served under Napoleon or had been in service with other European powers. Some Sonderbund officers had been members of the Swiss regiments of the French Royal Guard, until those units had been disbanded after the revolution in France of 1830. Many officers had signed conventions with the kingdom of Naples, which country maintained a number of Swiss regiments.

Like the American Civil War fifteen years later, the troops were full of enthusiasm to protect their home canton, but the realities of even a short campaign were not what many had expected. Some desertions occurred in the Confederate cantons when Catholics refused to take up arms against their fellow religionists. Equally, some Sonderbund companies declined to march beyond their canton's boundaries, or refused to obey orders when commanded to attack the Confederates.

The army consisted of infantry, rifles, artillery, sappers, pontoon troops and cavalry. The basic unit in the infantry was the company, made up of four officers, 17 NCOs, one barber, one sapper, three signallers (drummers or buglers) and 99 men, together 125 men. Six companies made up a battalion, which had a staff of a lieutenant-colonel, a major and 16 non-combatants. Four of the companies were styled fusiliers and two jäger, in German, or chasseurs, in French. A rifle company, referred to as 'sharpshooters' in the Swiss orders of battle, consisted of four officers, 14 NCOs, one barber, one gunsmith, two buglers and 78 men. There was no larger formation. In practice, the number of

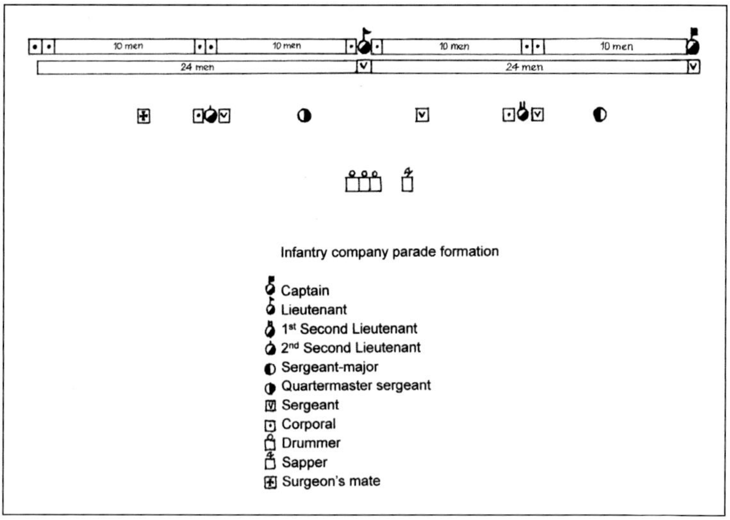

The formation of an infantry company. (Ralph Weaver)

personnel in an infantry company varied between 114 and 141, depending upon the canton. Also, the number of companies in each battalion was not uniform. There were 59 battalions of six companies and 15 with five companies. In the smaller battalions only one company was designated as a 'light' company.

An artillery company had four officers, one surgeon, 14 NCOs, one barber, four professional gunners, two drummers and 45 men. Each battery had four guns. Each battery also had its own train under an officer. The sapper and pontoon companies had four officers, 10 NCOs, one barber, two drummers and 54 men. The cavalry companies, styled either dragoons or guides, consisted of three officers, 10 NCOs, one barber, one vet, one smith, one saddle maker, two trumpeters and 45 troopers.

Not all cantons had exactly the same system, but the military strength was based on young men between the ages of twenty and twenty-five called to the 'Standing or Elite contingent', in which they served for a period of three years, before they then moved to the Reserve for a further three years. After that term they were enrolled in the 'Landwehr' for another three years, and afterwards remained liable to be called out in the home guard, or the 'Landsturm' until they reached the age of sixty. Both elite and reserve constituted the formal strength of the army – in the 1830s each category numbered 33,758, a total of over 67,000 men. Not all cantons had the same organisation. In Luzern men served in the Elite Contingent from the ages of 21 to 27; in the Landwehr from 27 to 48 and the Landsturm between the ages of 17 to 20 and from 49 to 60. Some cantons kept men in the Landsturm until they were 65.

The total force was made up of 74 'Elite' infantry battalions; 46 companies of riflemen; eight companies of mounted Guides; 24 companies of dragoons; 30 artillery companies; six sapper and two pontoon companies. Also included in the order of battle were 31 Reserve infantry battalions and 26 Reserve rifle companies. The cantons could also call upon men who had left the reserve companies and entered the Landwehr.

All this was controlled by a General Staff of 23 colonels; 17 lieutenant-colonels; 19 majors; 41 captains termed staff adjutants as opposed to company commanders and an

General William-Henry Dufour, commander of the Confederate forces. (Author's collection)

Colonel Ochsenbein, commander of the Bern Reserve Division and President of the Swiss Diet. (Author's collection)

equal number of lieutenants. It will be noted that there were no generals! These were appointed by the Federal Diet as occasion arose. These staff officers had the title 'Federal' before their rank to distinguish them from canton (part-time) officers.

Each 'Elite' infantry battalion was allotted a number, which ran from 1 to 74, irrespective of canton, number 1 came from Bern; 2 from Tessin; 3 from Zurich; 4 from Aargau etc.[1] The rifle companies were also numbered from 1 to 46, again irrespective of canton. Number 1 was raised in Bern; 2 from Zurich; 3 from Waadt; 4 from Bern etc.[2] The mounted guide companies were numbered 1 to 8 and the dragoons had their own numbered sequence. Artillery companies and sappers were also numbered. When the individual companies were formed into battalions, brigades and divisions, they were all named for their commanding officer before their allocated number. For example, in the Confederation army, Battalion Benz was battalion number 11 from Zurich, part of Egloff's Brigade of Ziegler's Fourth Division. In the Sonderbund army Company Ottiger was part of Battalion Meyer-Bielmann of Schmid's 3rd Brigade of Ruttimann's 1st Division. Hopefully the staff officers carried a full order of battle with them!

The army of the Confederation raised for the disbandment of the Sonderbund was organised into brigades, each of three battalions plus a rifle company, a cavalry company and several artillery companies. Three brigades made up a division. In 1847 the Swiss Confederation mustered seven divisions, together with reserves, of over 98,000 men and 172 pieces of artillery. The Sonderbund army put four divisions into the field. Together

1 See Appendix VIII for a complete list.
2 See Appendix IX for a complete list.

Colonel Frederick Rillet-Constant, commander of the Confederate First Division. (Author's collection)

Colonel Gmür, commander of the Confederate Fifth Division. (Author's collection)

with reserves and home guard this gave a total of over 34,000 men, although with less than 40 guns.

While the numbers, especially in the Confederation army, were impressive, the forces when assembled, were less so. Organisation, as planned by the General Staff, was excellent, but the training of the troops left something to be desired. In 1847 few men, if any, had been under fire; it was one thing to hunt in the mountains, or to take part in shooting contests, it was quite another to maintain discipline and morale under musket and artillery fire. It was true that some officers had served in other armies, in the Netherlands and particularly central and southern Italy, but they had not seen much, if any, action.

The Confederation had, over the years, been aware of the potential shortcomings of its troops and books and pamphlets were written on how to organise and train the canton forces. Each year the cantons called out their 'Elite' companies and spent a week or two in large training camps, sometimes numbering several thousand men. The weapons of the day demanded tight formations and fire discipline which could only be perfected in the large conscript or professional armies in Europe. While the Swiss knew in theory what was required, it was quite another thing to bring the companies up to the standard needed in the field. One of the reasons put forward by military observers during the conflict for the low numbers of casualties, was that the men fired at too great a distance and did not aim properly, many bullets going over the heads of opposing formations.

Most of the Swiss infantry, of both sides in the conflict, were similarly armed with a musket, the model 1817, modified 1842, which was the French model 1777 flintlock converted to percussion. This was meant to be the standard firearm, but as ever in Switzerland, each canton was free to purchase arms as they saw fit. The only agreement was on the calibre, which was 18mm. The model 1842 had a hardwood stock with a steel percussion lock. There seem to have been slight variations between the cantons, most had steel or iron barrel bands and fittings. It was fitted with a triangular socket bayonet, which was carried in a sheath attached to the ammunition pouch when not fixed. The muskets were imported from France after the Napoleonic Wars, the modification was made in factories in Switzerland. Other weapons were purchased from factories in Belgium, Liège companies supplying arms to most of Europe. Fusiliers did not carry a sidearm, only the chasseur companies had a short hanger, similar to contemporary German models.

The rifle companies carried a good quality rifled musket, which had a better accuracy than the fusilier firearm, but took longer to load as the ball and charge had to be hammered down the barrel. It was not a conversion, but built to the percussion standard. Riflemen carried a short sword as well as a bayonet.

The Landwehr were similarly armed and equipped to the Elite and Reserve companies, while the Landsturm brought with them anything they could lay their hands on. In canton Freiburg this could be firearms such as hunting rifles and shotguns or medieval pole-arms – pikes, spears, halberds and the famous Swiss weapon, the 'morning star'. This fearsome home-made club had a long handle with spikes protruding from the club end, devastating in close-quarter fighting. Fortunately, in the attack on Freiburg, there was little action involving the home guards.

The three cantons of Basel-Stadt, Appenzell (Inner) and Neuenburg remained neutral, but as they counted only about 3,000 men between them, they had no effect on the overall balance. Basel-Stadt and Appenzell (Inner) had strong Catholic minorities

Confederate troops prepare to march. (Author's collection)

who they did not want to antagonise and Neuenburg was technically a Prussian province and had been advised not to get involved.

In 1707, on the death of the childless French Princess of Neuenburg the canton council looked for a new head of state. They had to be Protestant and powerful enough to ensure they would not be swamped by any neighbouring power. From the more than a dozen claimants they chose Frederick I of Prussia. He fulfilled the criteria with the added bonus of being far enough away to let them get on with the business of government without too much interference.

As in the Sonderbund, the Confederation had to select a 'general' to take command of the forces under its control. They selected the most senior Federal colonel, Dufour, who eventually accepted the position. He was an expert administrator and within a couple of weeks had organised the Confederation forces into six divisions, irrespective of canton. This seemed an enormous number of men for the task of subduing the smaller Sonderbund armies, but Dufour wanted no doubt that the Confederation army was serious in its appointed task. He informed the Confederation Diet that only by using overwhelming numbers could he guarantee success. He also stressed to the council and his own assembled troops that they would be fighting fellow Swiss and that he did not wish to see the horrors associated with civil war visited upon the country. As proof of his intensions, when offered Congreve rockets from an armoury, he refused to add them to his artillery as he thought them too indiscriminately destructive.

4

The Campaign opens – Aargau

While Dufour was concentrating his forces around Freiburg, the Sonderbund commander decided on a bold stroke hoping to distract the Confederation plans. General Salis-Soglio took a column of Luzern troops over the border into canton Aargau. Across the River Reuss the district of Aargau, called the Freiamt, was largely peopled by Catholic farmers who had some sympathy with the Sonderbund. If he could detach this area from the Confederation it would be a major success.

On 12 November Salis-Soglio sent a small column against the village of Capel in canton Zurich, to mask his real intentions, while he led four battalions of infantry, a company of riflemen and two batteries of artillery against a pontoon bridge near the village of Lunnern. The morning was foggy, which helped the Luzerners approach the

Troops of the Confederate Second Division at rest during a march, 12 November 1847. The sketch was drawn by Lieutenant Charles-Alexandre Steinhäuslin, a member of the 1st Company, 19th Battalion, 2nd Brigade of the Fourth Division. He made a series of fine pen and ink drawings of the campaign that are reproduced throughout this book, based both on his own experiences and the testimony of others. (Steinhäuslin, *Bilder aus dem Sonderbundskriege im November 1847*, 1848)

Confederate troops skirmishing at the engagement of Lunnern, 12 November 1847. (Steinhäuslin, *Bilder aus dem Sonderbundskriege im November 1847*, 1848)

pontoon bridge unobserved. Just in time they were discovered and the defenders had enough warning to dismantle part of the bridge. The Luzern troops advanced to the riverbank and opened fire on the Zurich troops defending the bridge works. These were part of Colonel Gmür's Division, Meyer's battalion, No.29, Huber's company of Riflemen and Scheller's 6 pounder battery. They were later joined by some companies from Fäsi's battalion, Ziegler's Division.

The two sides fired across the river at each other for some time, inflicting a small numbers of casualties. One lucky shot from Scheller's battery dismounted one of the Sonderbund guns. Not so lucky for the Luzern soldiers on the river bank was the presence of Rifleman Jacques Spörri who, taking cover behind a large oak tree by the riverbank, managed to bring down a number of Sonderbunders by taking careful aim. Even when wounded in the knee as a result of cannon fire, he continued to fire until wounded a second time.

Unable to get across the river, Salis-Soglio had no option but to retire. His second-in-command, Colonel Elgger, had in the meantime advanced further downriver to the village of Geltwill and put to flight two companies of Aargau infantry from Berner's Battalion No.42. During this small action an officer on each side was killed and Elgger's young son, who was acting as his father's aide-de-camp, was wounded. Although Elgger was able to keep possession of Geltwill, he was forced to return to Luzern as Salis-Soglio's retirement had left him unsupported. The fighting had lasted several hours and the fire

The action at Geltwyl, 12 November 1847. The figure on the left, in cocked hat, is Prince Schwarzenberg, a leading Sonderbund commander. (Author's collection)

of the guns had been heard in Zurich many miles away. Typically for the war the number of casualties was comparatively small – at Lunnern two men were killed and 10 wounded on the Confederate side and probably a similar figure for the Sonderbund (although no records seem to have been kept, other than for canton Luzern) and at Geltwill, the Confederates suffered one officer and two men killed and 15 wounded, the Luzerners losing two killed, one being Lieutenant Schnyder, who was the only cavalryman to become a casualty, and four wounded.

5

The Confederation takes the initiative – Freiburg

With his engineering and map-making background Dufour quickly saw that the Sonderbund was made up of a number of states separated by Confederation territory. Luzern and the old Swiss cantons formed one block, with Freiburg isolated to the west. Wallis was joined to Uri but a mountain ridge blocked easy access. Dufour's plan was relatively simple: mass the bulk of the Confederation army on the borders of Freiburg and strike against its small army before the Luzern and central Sonderbund states could come to its aid. With Freiburg defeated, the army would move against the centre of Sonderbund power in Luzern.

The commander of the Freiburg army, François Philippe de Maillardoz, raised an impressive number of troops to defend the canton, on paper at least. The total of 23,250 men was however largely made up of 7,160 Second Landwehr and 10,066 Landsturm. The most reliable troops were the Elite contingent of 3,026 men and the First Landwehr of 2,443, not enough when faced with the whole Confederation army.

Bivouac of Confederate troops in the environs of Freiburg, 13 November 1847. (Steinhäuslin, *Bilder aus dem Sonderbundskriege im November 1847*, 1848)

The Freiburg army was organised in three brigades, besides a small force dedicated as the garrison of Freiburg city. This consisted of the City Guard Company of 70 men, 200 Landwehr of the second class and 20 gendarmes.

The First brigade was commanded by Colonel Schaller with the 2nd Battalion of the Elite contingent under Lieutenant-colonel Appenthel and Major Bondallez (each battalion was divided into two half battalions), the 1st Battalion of Landwehr under Lieutenant-colonel Weck and Major Vonderweid-Hattenberg, the 1st Company of Elite Riflemen, and one officer and 12 dragoons of the Landwehr cavalry.

The second brigade, under Colonel Albiez, contained the 1st Battalion of the Elite contingent under Lieutenant-colonel Castella and Major Eggar, the 2nd Battalion of the Landwehr under Lieutenant-colonel Müller and Major Landerset, and the 2nd company of Riflemen. They were accompanied by 12 Landwehr dragoons.

The third brigade, commanded by Colonel Moret, contained the 3rd Elite Battalion under Lieutenant-colonel Caille and Major Reynold, the 3rd Landwehr Battalion under Lieutenant-colonel Gottrau and Major Féguely, and the 1st Company of Landwehr Riflemen. One officer and 12 Landwehr dragoons completed the brigade.

Not attached to the three brigades were the 2nd Company of Landwehr Riflemen, the remainder of the Landwehr dragoons (13 men) and the Elite cavalry contingent of 96 men. The artillery had a compliment of 280 men and comprised four 8-pounders;

The Confederate Second Division near Belfaux, 14 November 1847. (Steinhäuslin, *Bilder aus dem Sonderbundskriege im November 1847*, 1848)

eight 6-pounders, 14 4-pounders, six 24-pound howitzers, one 12-pound howitzer and two mortars, 33 guns in all. There were also two mountain howitzers on the strength.

Maillardoz' only plan was to make the best defence of the city as he possibly could. He hoped to delay any attack on his canton and wait for help from Luzern and the central Swiss cantons. To this end a number of forts were constructed around the city of Freiburg, it being impossible to try to defend all the borders of the canton. The real threat appeared to be from the canton Bern to the east, so the 1st and 2nd Brigades were positioned outside the city facing the perceived threat on the right bank of the River Saane. The city sat on the left bank of the river with the 3rd Brigade facing west behind a line of three redoubts positioned on high ground. These redoubts covered the roads leading from canton Waadt to the city of Freiburg. Each was equipped with artillery and supporting infantry and with further infantry posted in support. A number of earthworks, all built by convict labour, were erected in front of the forts and manned by the Landsturm.

The first part of Dufour's plan of campaign was to mass as many men as possible against Freiburg and to capture the city before any troops from other cantons could come to its aid. He hoped that his large army would intimidate the Freiburg council into surrendering without a fight. The first Confederation troops crossed the frontier into Freiburg canton on 7 November, and by 13 November three divisions surrounded

Confederate troops in cantonments, November 1847. (Steinhäuslin, *Bilder aus dem Sonderbundskriege im November 1847*, 1848)

the city. The Bern Reserve Division under Colonel Ulrich Ochsenbein (he represented the canton of Bern in the Swiss Diet, and at this time was President of the Swiss Federal Government) approached Freiburg on the right of the river where it faced the 1st and 2nd Brigades, but the 3rd Brigade faced overwhelming numbers from the Confederation First and Second Divisions plus Brigade Hauser from Third Division and Brigade Müller from Fourth Division.

Early that morning Dufour sent a staff officer to Freiburg to speak to the council and ask them to surrender in order to save unnecessary loss of life. The council asked for a 24 hour armistice to consider the terms, which Dufour was happy to grant as he could use the time profitably to bring up more troops. Unfortunately, news of the truce did not reach all the Confederate units and a skirmish broke out near one of the forts, at Bertigny. The Confederates of Rillet's First Division were caught in the open and the Freiburgers, firing from their entrenchments, inflicted seven dead and wounded 50.

Although this successful defence of the fort raised the morale of the Freiburg troops and citizens, it did not alter the fact that their situation was desperate. The council members could see the Confederation troops all round the city and responded to Dufour that they were ready to capitulate. The terms were harsh, forcing them to lay down their arms, withdraw from the Sonderbund and elect a new council. There was really no choice – Freiburg duly surrendered and Confederate troops marched in and occupied the city.

The knock-on effect of Freiburg's surrender was to weaken the resolve of canton Zug, which had not been overwhelmingly in favour of the Sonderbund from the start. On 20 November Dufour received word that Zug also was ready to surrender, without seeing a single Confederation soldier. The first part of Dufour's plan had worked almost without a hitch, except for the fighting before Bertigny. He now reorganised his forces for the next move.

6

The Attack on Luzern

As Dufour gathered his army for the attack on Luzern, a small detachment of Sonderbund troops from the contingents of Schwyz and Zug crossed the frontier of Luzern into Zurich at the village of Knonau. Battalion Brunner (Zurich No.3) of the first brigade of Gmür's Fifth Division was stationed here and repulsed the attack. The Sonderbunders fell back on Steinhausen in the canton of Zug (the frontiers of the three cantons met in the area), closely followed by Brunner. It is reported that the action lasted for some hours, yet Confederate records show that their only casualty was Fusilier Schlumpf of the 3rd Company, whose left arm was grazed by a ball.

The canton of Luzern was the most important part of the Sonderbund. It had a large population, a strong army and the leader of the Luzern council, Constantin Siegwart-Müller, was the political head of the Sonderbund. Dufour calculated that by removing Luzern from his list of opponents, the rest would quickly capitulate. He used the same strategy that he had used against Freiburg, bringing massive forces against the Luzern army, in the hope that they would decide not to make a fight of it. He knew the strengths of his opponents' forces and even if all the troops of the small cantons joined with Luzern, he could bring overwhelming numbers against them. He was also intending

Confederate troops in bivouac before Luzern. (Author's collection)

to use all the roads leading to the city of Luzern, without disguising his intentions, to intimidate the defenders.

The forces detailed for the march on Luzern (as Dufour hoped it would be) were the Second, Third, Fourth, Fifth and Bern Reserve divisions. Of his other forces, First Division was marching south from Freiburg against the canton of Wallis and Sixth Division was defending the canton Tessin against a small incursion from Sonderbund troops.

Dufour issued an order to his army to the effect that even as they were entering enemy territory they were to do their duty without rancour, be assured of victory and treat the defeated with kindness and indulgence. This was hardly a rousing call to action, but demonstrated Dufour's concern that no unnecessary bloodshed or destruction take place and that churches and private property were to be respected.

The Confederation forces set out on the morning of 22 November, each division taking one of the five main roads leading to the city of Luzern. Von Donats' Third Division was to advance directly from the north by the town of Sursee; Burkhardt's Second Division from the north-west by Hutwyl and Willisau; the Bern Reserve Division, under Colonel Ochsenbein, by the Entlebuch valley from the south-west. The two eastern roads were assigned to Colonel Ziegler's Fourth Division by the towns of Muri and Münster, and Gmür's Fifth Division from Zurich around the lake of Zug. The roads taken by Fourth and Fifth divisions came together at the bridge by the village of Gisikon and from there the direct route lay alongside the River Reuss. Dufour anticipated that this would be the site of any action, as this was the most open route to the city and the Luzern authorities had constructed several batteries and redoubts between the river and the high ground to cover the bridge and its approaches.

Each division was sent orders, and on Sunday 21st the Bern Reserve Division under Colonel Ochsenbein was given its orders to march on Luzern by the valley of the Entlebuch and the village of Langnau and the town of Schüpfheim. It was envisaged that it would arrive before the city of Luzern by the 24th. The difficulty of the advance was quickly demonstrated by the slow progress down a narrow valley, between thickly wooded heights. The first unit began its march at 9 o'clock in the morning, with the last troops not moving until 11pm. Ochsenbein had ready to hand six battalions of infantry, six companies of rifles, two companies of dragoons, one company of sappers and 16 four-pounder guns in four companies of artillery, a total of 6,000 men. A further 6-700 Landwehr were posted at Langnau.

The column was led by an advance guard under Lieutenant-colonel Brugger, made up of Jäger companies Schneider and Jung from the 3rd and 4th Battalions, Rifle Company Klopfenstein, 20 sappers under Lieutenant Wyttenbach with the 5th Company of the 2nd Battalion under Major Wyss in reserve, altogether 1,100 men. They were greeted by a few shots from the local militia, from high above the road, who quickly disappeared when riflemen from Klopfenstein's company chased after them. They found a guard post unoccupied, but with a signal fire ready to be lit. A section of riflemen under Lieutenant Karlen followed a path until they came to a view down the valley where they could make out a force of 800 to 1,000 men waiting for them. They were mostly militia but there were about 200 regulars among them, judging by the uniforms.

As the advance guard approached the village of Escholzmatt they were fired on, but the shooting was at long range and had no effect. At the outskirts of the village a group

Troops from the Confederate Second Division enter Luzern on 22 November 1847. (Steinhäuslin, *Bilder aus dem Sonderbundskriege im November 1847*, 1848)

Confederate troops halted during operations around Luzern, 22 November 1847. (Steinhäuslin, *Bilder aus dem Sonderbundskriege im November 1847*, 1848)

Confederate artillery is brought into action during the combat at Schüpfheim, 23 November 1847. (Steinhäuslin, *Bilder aus dem Sonderbundskriege im November 1847*, 1848)

The bivouac of Confederate Battalion Kistler, 23-24 November 1847. (Steinhäuslin, *Bilder aus dem Sonderbundskriege im November 1847*, 1848)

of citizens appeared with a white flag, while the Luzern troops retreated along the valley. The Bern troops, with some encouragement, advanced through the village and beyond. Although no Sonderbund troops were found, the Bernese discovered several roadblocks, which they had to dismantle before proceeding. At Schüpfheim, the main town of the valley, the Luzern troops made a stand. In the early hours of the 23rd they opened fire on the Confederates, killing one and wounding 20. The men from Bern again hesitated and it took Ochsenbein himself to shame his troops into renewing their attack. He also brought up his artillery to bombard the Sonderbund positions. The Luzern records show that they lost 15 men killed and a further nine wounded in the action.

The Luzerners fell back before them, fearful of being outflanked by the Bern Rifle Company of Captain Moser. It may also be that their artillery had run out of ammunition! Nothing could now stop the Bernese and as they advanced on Luzern, a number of fortified positions were encountered, which were either unmanned or the garrisons had hastily withdrawn. Broken bridges were repaired and a mine, a barrel of gunpowder buried beneath the road, was defused. They arrived at the city of Luzern on the 24th, as planned.

7

The Battle of Gisikon (or Gislikon)

A Prussian military historian and former officer, Friedrich Wilhelm Rüstow, writing about the battle of Gisikon (or Gislikon, as it is also referred to), derided much of the then current accounts as 'pompous'. To him it resembled nothing more than a battle in miniature. This was because of the small number of casualties sustained by both sides, caused by the troops firing too high, as was to be seen after the battle, when many Confederate troops could show broken bayonets and injured shakos but very few killed and wounded. There were several reasons for this. The soldiers were inexperienced. Although they may have been good hunters and marksmen, that did not make for efficient fire tactics in the field (deer or hares in the mountains never shoot back!) The country was not good for artillery, with the ground broken up by hills, patches of woodland, small villages and isolated farms. When artillery was used it tried to make up for any deficiency by firing as rapidly as possible. A few chance shots appear to have been enough to cause panic among the troops – one Sonderbund battalion broke and ran after a single 12-pounder shot passed through them, causing no more than a dozen casualties.

General Salis-Soglio assembled his forces between the River Reuss, and the Rooterberg, which form a chain of heights between two lakes, the higher region being

The Battle of Gisikon. (Author's collection)

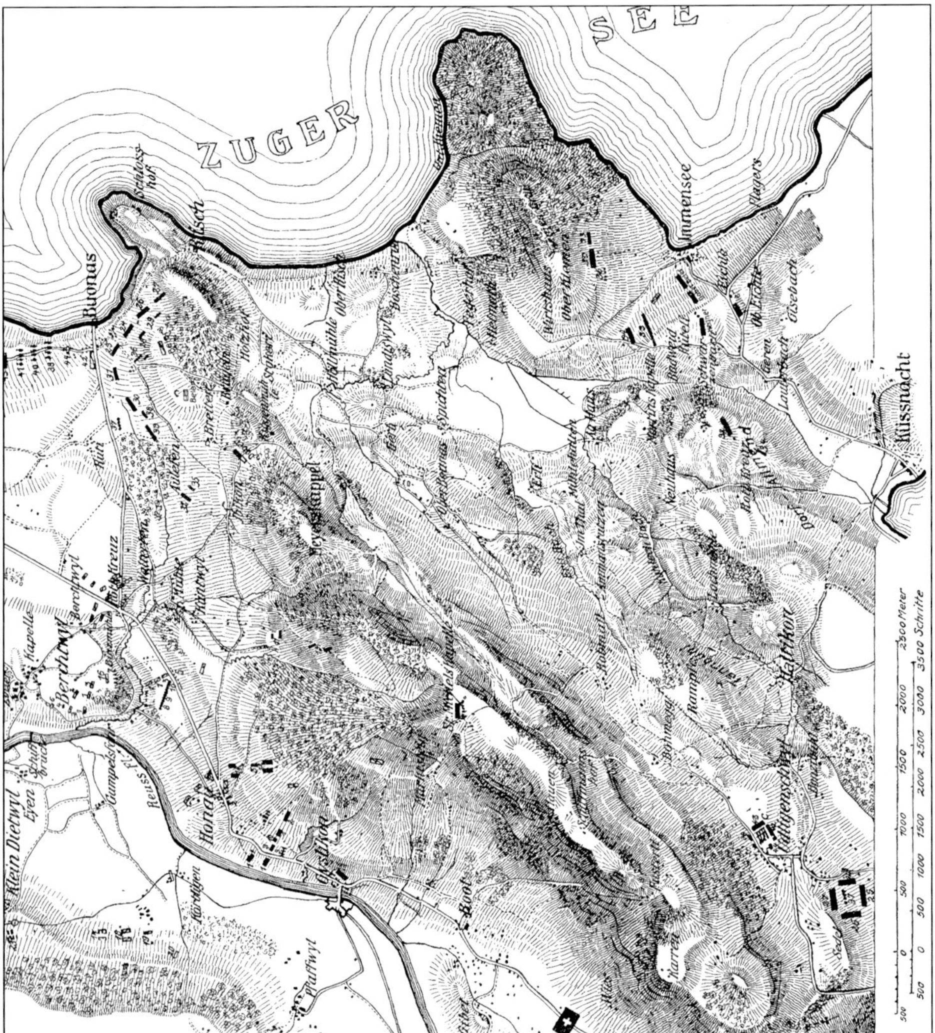

Plan of the Battle of Gisikon/Meierskappel, 23 November 1847. (Author's collection)

thickly studded with fir trees. The forces of Luzern were stationed on both banks of the Reuss, well provided with artillery and riflemen, while the mountain itself was occupied by a strong body of regular troops and armed peasantry. The object of the troops of the Sonderbund was clear; the attack of the Confederates on both sides of the Rooterberg was to be stopped at any price, and possession kept of the road leading to Luzern. However, at this moment, the commander of the Schwyz contingent took it upon himself to withdraw his men from the field in order to defend a pass leading into the western part of his canton. The Confederate troops, as might have been expected, soon took advantage of this mistake and occupied without the loss of a single man, a position which they ought to have been made to purchase dearly.

Dufour concentrated the Fourth Division in the area between the river and the Rooterberg, facing towards the village of Honau, with Gisikon as the objective. The latter village sat on the banks of the river, where several main roads converged, and had a large covered bridge spanning the river. The Luzern authorities had built several battery positions covering the bridge and the approaches to it. The river valley was very narrow in places, which made it difficult for both sides to deploy their forces fully.

Four further divisions were closing in on the city of Luzern from every direction. The Fifth Division of Colonel Gmür, after capturing the town of Zug on 20 November, advanced from the canton of Zug, along the shore of the lake (also called Zug Lake) and approached the Rooterberg, aiming towards the village of Meierskappel. The Third Division marched through difficult country from the west, the Second Division was almost parallel, but headed towards Luzern city from the south.

On the night of the 22nd the Fourth Division made camp on the frontier of canton Luzern and, across the Reuss, could see the campfires of the Fifth Division. Early the following morning, under cover of a thick fog, men of the Aargau pontoon company Number 2, Captain Vögtli, built several pontoon bridges across the river over which marched the 1st Brigade Egloff followed by the 2nd Brigade König. As soon as they were across the river, the fog lifted and the Confederates saw the Sonderbund troops lining hedges and behind farmhouses on higher ground. Müller's 3rd Brigade was detailed to attack the Gisikon bridge from the other side of the river; it should have been the Third Division, but they had been held up on the bad roads and did not arrive in time to take part in the battle. Müller's troops were shaken by artillery fire and temporarily retired.

The first part of the battle consisted of the artillery batteries of each side trying to make their opponents disengage. The early advantage was gained by the Confederates, who forced the Sonderbund guns to pull back from Honau to Gisikon. One Sonderbund battery, commanded by Captain Mazzola, stood firm at Gisikon and held the advancing Confederates at bay. At this point it seems that the Confederate artillery battery of 6-pounder guns under Captain Rust took it upon themselves to rectify the situation by galloping through their own infantry and unlimber only 500 yards (about 450 metres) from Mazzola's position. They exchanged fire for sometime before Rust, observing some Luzern riflemen trying to cut him off, ordered his battery to retire.

As the battery withdrew, Mazzola was aware of a body of troops close by, but the smoke and dust made it impossible to make out who they were. Artillery corporal Pfiffer volunteered to take a look. As he crossed a field he made out the Federal flags and ran back to the battery shouting, 'Fire, Captain! It's the enemy!" The nearest unit was Häusler's Elite Battalion No.15 from Aargau, who began to waver under the fire of

Engagement at Honau, an episode during the Battle of Gisikon. (Steinhäuslin, *Bilder aus dem Sonderbundskriege im November 1847,* 1848)

Mazzola's guns. Major Scherrer took hold of the battalion colour and stuck the staff into the ground, shouting to the men to stand alongside the flag. His bold action saved the situation and the battalion held firm.

Colonel Ziegler's Division had succeeded in linking up with the right wing of the Fifth division of Colonel Gmür. The storming of the enemy's position on the Rooterberg was undertaken by Brigade König, which was supported by the fire of Schweizer's 12-pounder battery. The Sonderbunders were driven from their positions and the Confederates, in spite of the fire of the enemy's artillery, advanced on Gisikon. This was the crown of the position of the Sonderbunders; their strongly entrenched batteries commanded both banks of the Reuss, the lower batteries also commanded the highway to Luzern, and the trenches built on the mountain were defended by the riflemen of Unterwalden. On the summit of the mountain were posted the 'Landsturm' or armed peasantry, and the approaches to these works were protected by barricades formed of masses of stone, and the trunks of trees.

Despite the heavy fire kept up by the Sonderbunders; the Confederates continued to advance towards Gisikon, and the former for some time made a show of defending the position to the last. The Confederates made some gains in ground but then were forced back. Ziegler himself came forward to see what was holding up the attack. At this critical moment he dismounted from his horse, stood at the head of the Battalion Ginsberg, ordered the drummers to beat 'the charge' and led them in a bayonet attack which began the eventual collapse of the Sonderbund resistance. It was clear that it

Action near the bridge of Gisikon, during the battle (Steinhäuslin, *Bilder aus dem Sonderbundskriege im November 1847*, 1848)

was not the number of casualties that caused the Sonderbunders to withdraw, but the low morale of some units. Here politics played its part on the battlefield – many of the Luzern defenders had little sympathy with their government, certainly not enough to lose their lives defending it.

The brigade of Colonel König continued its successful advance onto the Rooterberg until it came upon the Michelscappel, a chapel on the crest of the ridge. This was strongly held and the defenders would not budge. It was only the appearance of Gmür's Division in their rear that caused them to break off the fight. Gmür had taken the Sonderbund position at Meierskappel and was now advancing along the road towards Luzern City.

While the fight before Gisikon was swaying back and forth, Gmür's Division was climbing the hills on the south side of the Rooterberg. At the outset of the battle Brigade Ritter had been acting in support of Ziegler at Honau, and now moved against the Rooterberg in conjunction with Brigade Isler, supported by a battery of artillery. It was a hard slog as they were advancing uphill with the Sonderbunders shooting down on them. It was here that Captain Frauenfelder, leading the 1st company of chasseurs from Battalion Brunner received a ball in the thigh from a Schwyz rifleman from which he later died.

The Confederates fell back for a while, until Brunner, supported by riflemen from Appenzell and Graubunden, led a second assault up the hill. This time they kept coming and the Sonderbunders fell back before them. The latter desperately sent messages for help, but no-one came to their aid. In the end superior numbers told and the Confederates

Colonel Ziegler, commander of the Fourth Division in the Confederate army. (Author's collection)

Colonel Ziegler leads Battalion Ginsberg, Confederate army, to the attack at Gisikon. (Author's collection)

Combat for the Rooterberg at Gisikon. (Steinhäuslin, *Bilder aus dem Sonderbundskriege im November 1847*, 1848)

Combat near a redoubt at Gisikon. (Steinhäuslin, *Bilder aus dem Sonderbundskriege im November 1847*, 1848)

Battery Moll, from the Confederate army, in action during the Battle of Gisikon. (Steinhäuslin, *Bilder aus dem Sonderbundskriege im November 1847*, 1848)

at last gained the village of Meierskappel. Some of the Sonderbund troops took shelter in the church and from the tower continued to fire until an artillery piece put a cannon ball through the structure. From then the retreat gained momentum, with the remaining Schwyz troops marching back to their own canton and the others falling back hurriedly on the city of Luzern.

With the collapse of the Meierskappel position the Sonderbund 1st Division of Colonel Ruttiman was in danger of being taken in flank and rear. His own position at Gisikon was being pressed back and Salis-Soglio realised that he could not hold the line any longer At 3 o'clock he gave orders to fall back on the village of Ebikon, which was about three miles (five kilometers) from Luzern. There was little point in taking up a new position as the Confederates were pressing forward on all sides, the other columns approaching Luzern from every direction.

There were still some officers who argued for further action, Salis-Soglio's adjutant, the Austrian Prince Schwarzenberg, making strong representations. He tried to persuade the commander in chief that there were a number of battalions of infantry and some rifle companies who had not been engaged and were thus capable of an effective defence. Salis-Soglio was not convinced and sent a message to the Luzern council that no further action could be of any purpose.

On the evening of the battle Colonel Ziegler sent a pencil note to General Dufour to inform him that his division was at the village of Root and that the bridge at Gisikon was open and passable from the north and west sides. The Confederate divisions now formed a semi-circle round the city of Luzern within a two hours' march of the city gates. In and

Rust's Confederate battery at Gisikon. (Author's collection)

around the city there were still about 20,000 Sonderbund troops, but with no plan for their further use.

Casualties recorded for the Confederate Fourth Division for the battle were 14 killed and 84 wounded. As the division fielded over 9,000 men, with a further 7,000 following in reserve, this was very light. Figures for the Sonderbund army are difficult to find, but their losses for the whole campaign were 26 dead and 140 wounded. These are the figures gathered and published by Dufour. The Luzern returns, however, name 40 men killed and 43 wounded for the whole war for their canton alone. 27 were either killed at Gisikon, or died of wounds either in hospital or before they could be treated. A further 27 men were listed as wounded. Among the casualties was the Sonderbund commander, General Salis-Soglio, who was struck in the head by a splinter from a cannon ball while observing the fight from Mazzola's battery. He continued to encourage his men, but soon had to retire to Luzern where the rest of the Luzern government fled to safety on a steamer across the lake. The Battle of Gisikon was the longest and the bloodiest of the war. It was the last pitched battle in the history of the Swiss army. It was also the first battle in military history in which dedicated wagons were employed to treat the wounded on the battlefield. These horse-drawn ambulances were operated by medical volunteers and nurses from Zürich.

8

The End of the War

On the evening of 23 November, Siegwart-Müller, the political head of the Sonderbund, together with members of his council, many Jesuit priests and the Sonderbund treasure chest, took a steamer from Luzern across the lake to the canton of Uri and then proceeded on foot to Wallis and finally across the Simplon Pass into Piedmont, or into Austrian-ruled Lombardy.

On the morning of the 24th, the City of Luzern council, Colonel Ab-Yberg, the commander of the troops of canton Schwyz, and General Salis-Soglio all sent a separate message to General Dufour requesting an armistice. On instructions from the Confederate government, Dufour refused and demanded unconditional surrender. Luzern immediately complied and to show its willingness, raised the Federal flag throughout the city. The Luzern troops were disbanded and those of Uri and Unterwalden were withdrawn into their own cantons. Around midday the Confederate troops entered

Confederate troops on the march in the days following their victory at Gisikon. (Steinhäuslin, *Bilder aus dem Sonderbundskriege im November 1847*, 1848)

Confederate troops on the march in the days following their victory at Gisikon. (Steinhäuslin, *Bilder aus dem Sonderbundskriege im November 1847*, 1848)

the city to be greeted with cheers and flowers. The occupation was generally peaceful apart from some looting of the empty houses of those Sonderbund leaders who had fled.

In Luzern, Dufour immediately wrote to the leaders of cantons of Uri, Schwyz and Unterwalden demanding their surrender. The last mentioned capitulated the following day, Schwyz on 26 November and Uri two days later. Dufour's plan of campaign to deal with Freiburg first and Luzern second had proved successful. As he had surmised, the smaller cantons had given up after the fall of Luzern. There remained the canton of Wallis. As early as the capture of Freiburg, as Dufour reorganised his troops for the attack on Luzern, he had detached the First Division, under Colonel Louis Rillet-Constant, to guard against incursions from Wallis. The division consisted of 10 battalions of infantry, six companies of riflemen, two companies of cavalry, two companies of sappers, a total force of 8,620 men together with 20 guns. He was ordered not to take any offensive action until Dufour had dealt with the major Sonderbund forces of Luzern and the central cantons.

Confederate troops pillaging, 25 November 1847. (Steinhäuslin, *Bilder aus dem Sonderbundskriege im November 1847*, 1848)

General Dufour and his staff enter Luzern, 28 November 1847. (Steinhäuslin, *Bilder aus dem Sonderbundskriege im November 1847*, 1848)

Federal staff officer. (Ralph Weaver)

Aargau fusilier, Confederate army. (Ralph Weaver)

Aargau officer. (Ralph Weaver)

Appenzell fusilier, Confederate army. (Ralph Weaver)

Solothurn artilleryman, Confederate army. (Ralph Weaver)

St Gallen fusilier, Confederate army. (Ralph Weaver)

Zurich fusilier, Confederate army. (Ralph Weaver)

Zurich fusilier NCO. (Ralph Weaver)

Zurich infantry drummer. (Ralph Weaver)

Zurich rifleman. (Ralph Weaver)

Zurich medical officer. (Ralph Weaver)

Luzern fusilier, Sonderbund army. (Ralph Weaver)

Luzern chasseur. (Ralph Weaver)

Freiburg Landsturm, armed with a lethal 'morning star', Sonderbund army. (Ralph Weaver)

Canton coats of arms. (Author's collection)

Canton badges, from Gautier's *Les Armoiries et les couleurs de la Confédération et des cantons suisses*, 1876. (via author)

Schwyz fusilier, Sonderbund army. (Ralph Weaver)

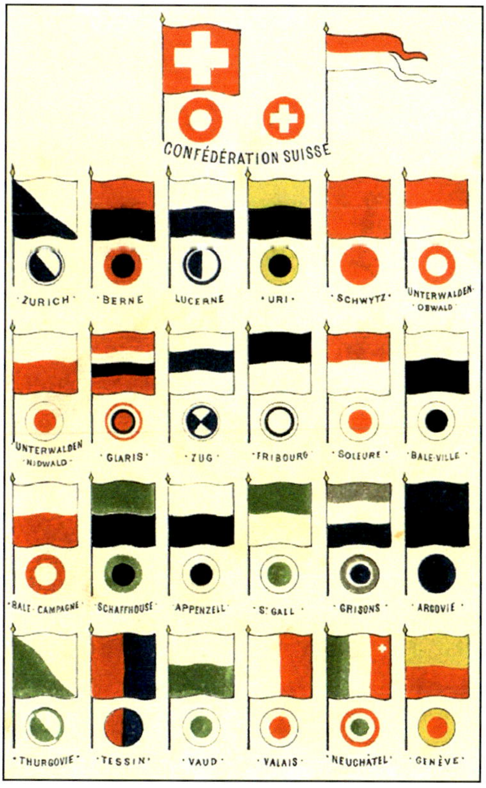

Canton colours and cockades, from Gautier's *Les Armoiries et les couleurs de la Confédération et des cantons suisses*, 1876. (via author)

Federal staff officers. A print after Albert von Escher. (Author's collection)

General Dufour, Confederate commander, and his staff. (Author's collection)

Appenzell infantry, Confederate army, in the uniform worn 1842-48. A print after von Escher. (Author's collection)

Bern infantry, Confederate army. A print after von Escher. (Author's collection)

An artillery unit from Bern as shown in a print after von Escher. (Author's collection)

St Gallen cavalryman, Confederate army. (Ron Poulter)

Rifle company officers from St Gallen, a rare contemporary photograph. (Swiss National Museum)

Tessin artillery, Confederate army, from a print after von Escher. (Author's collection)

'The good comrade' – Zurich Jägers, Confederate army, 1847, from a contemporary print. (Author's collection)

A naïve contemporary portrait of Corporal Franz Ermel, a drummer from Erlisbach, Zurich, Confederate army, painted in Luzern, December 1847. (Swiss National Museum)

Zurich engineers. (Author's collection)

Zurich dragoons, print after von Escher. (Author's collection)

Zurich volunteer.
(Ron Poulter)

The flag of Zurich, Confederate army, showing its dimensions. (Author's collection)

Aargau canton battle flag. (Ralph Weaver)

Schwyz infantry, Sonderbund army. A print after von Escher. (Author's collection)

Uri canton battle flag. (Ralph Weaver)

Canton Uri infantry, Sonderbund army. A print after von Escher. (Author's collection)

Zug artillery train troops, Sonderbund army, print after von Escher. (Author's collection)

The cannonade at the action of Lunnern, 12 November 1847. (Author's collection)

A canton Appenzell shako with bullet hole visible. The shako belonged to 24-year old Johann Jakob Knöpfel, who survived the Battle of Gisikon without injury! (Photo via author)

Two battle scenes, painted in a naïve style on the wall of a Freiburg farmhouse. (Author's collection)

Colonel Ziegler, commander of the Confederate Fourth Division, and staff, at Muri three days before the battle at Gisikon. (Author's collection)

Rust's Battery of the Confederate army at Gisikon in a watercolour by Albert von Escher. (Author's collection)

Confederate troops (Battalion Brunner) advancing at Meierskappel. In the middle distance can be seen Captain Frauenfelder, falling mortally wounded. (Author's collection)

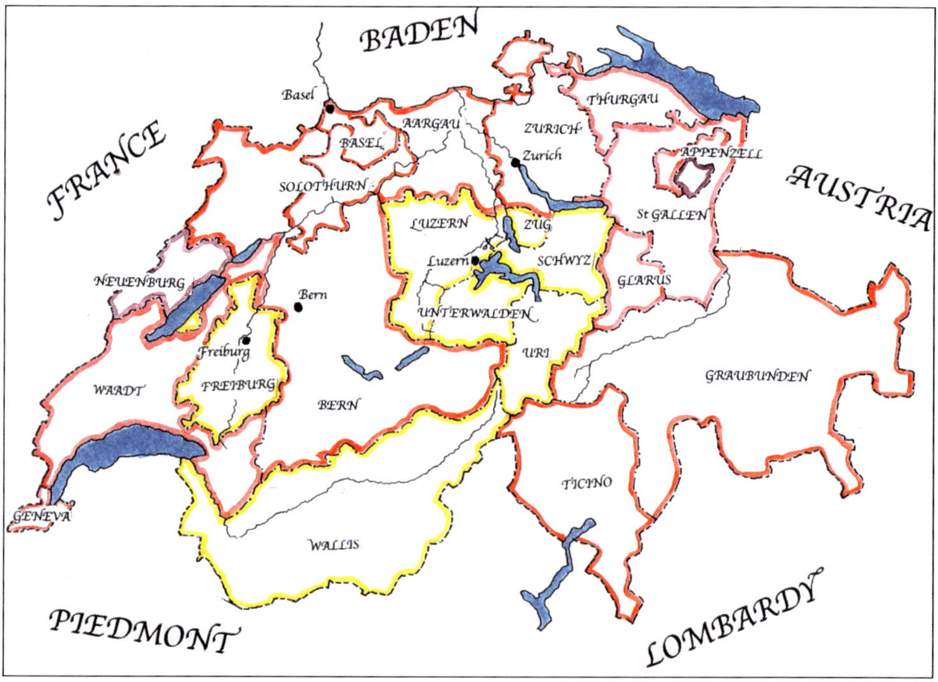

The Swiss cantons. Sonderbund cantons are bordered in yellow, Confederate cantons in red, neutral cantons in mauve. (Ralph Weaver)

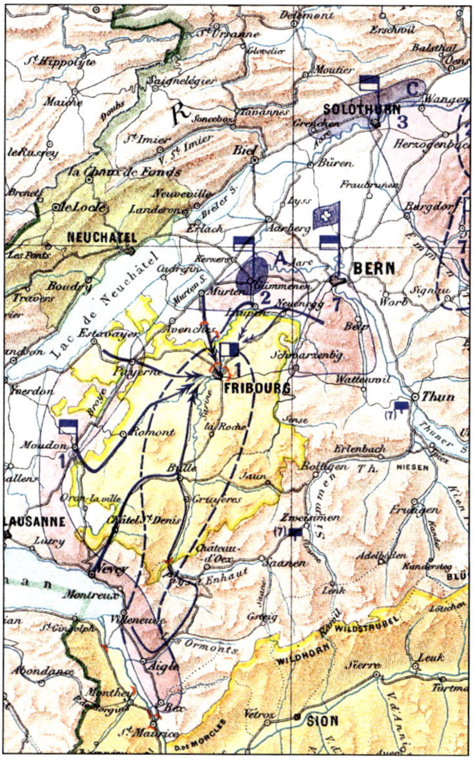

An overview of the campaign. (*Histoire Militaire de la Suisse* Tome 10, Bern, 1917)

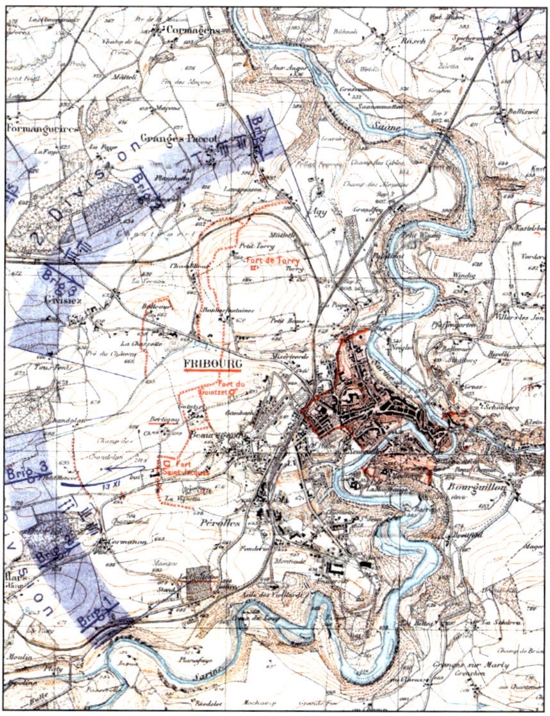

The Confederate forces approach Freiburg. (*Histoire Militaire de la Suisse* Tome 10, Bern, 1917)

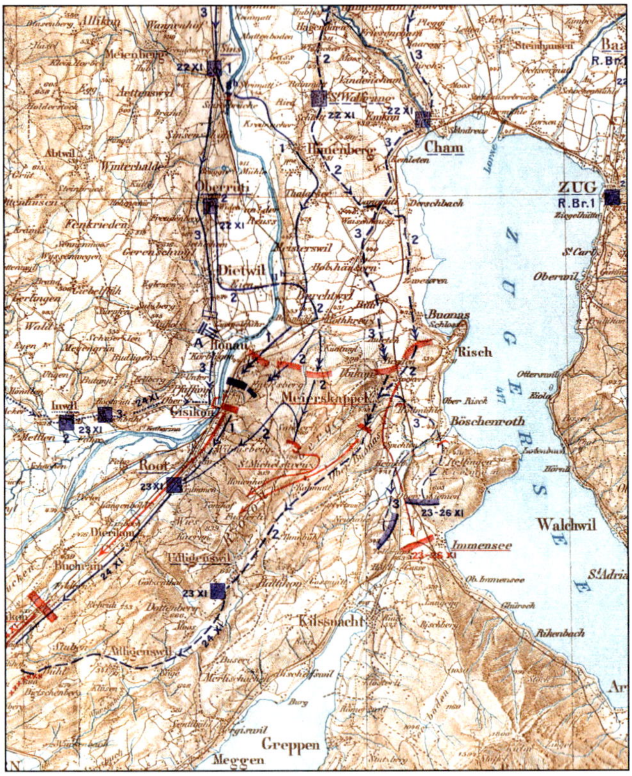

The campaign and battles at Gisikon and Meierskappel. (*Histoire Militaire de la Suisse* Tome 10, Bern, 1917)

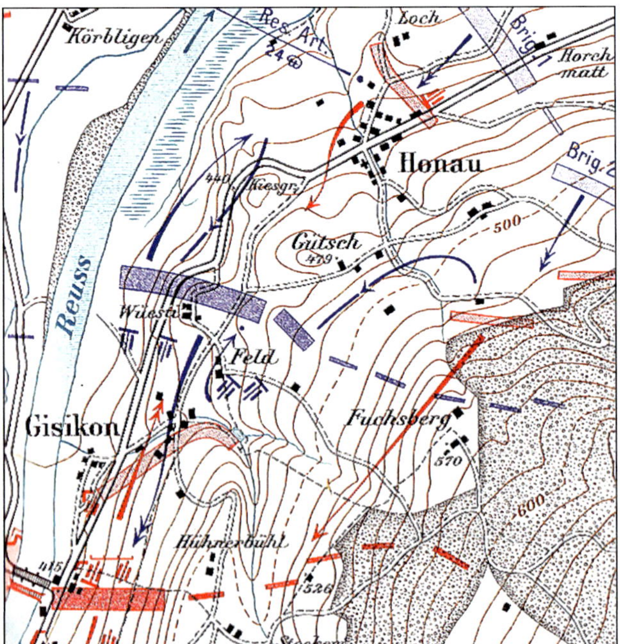

The Battle of Gisikon. (*Histoire Militaire de la Suisse* Tome 10, Bern, 1917)

9

The Last Act – Wallis

In Wallis the troops assembled by the canton military commander, General Wilhelm von Kalbermatten, were organised in three brigades, each consisting of two companies of sharpshooters, three battalions of infantry, and an artillery contingent with a total of eight guns. They were supported by a vast array of Landsturm men, 12,000 divided among rifle and infantry companies. The headquarters were in St Moritz. The geography of the canton is a long valley, narrow in places, surrounded by some of the highest mountains in Europe. In theory there were many places along the valley that could be easily defended by relatively small numbers of men and Dufour took this into account when ordering the First Division to keep a watching brief on the Wallis army while he dealt with Luzern.

Rillet-Constant, the commander of the Confederate forces, had instructions not to make any aggressive move until the Luzern army had been defeated or neutralised. As soon as the news of Gislikon had been received he made plans to advance into Wallis with his whole division. In numbers he had a slight overall advantage, but more of his men were 'Elite' or Reserve battalions. As soon as Dufour had reorganised his army he could send more troops against Wallis from the north. However the people of Wallis did not wait to be attacked and saw that their cause was now lost, making overtures of peace. These were accepted and the Confederate troops entered the last Sonderbund canton without having to fire a shot.

With the surrender of canton Wallis, the campaign was at an end. Most of the Confederation troops were demobilised to save money, except for the occupation forces of the former Sonderbund cantons. The first to leave were those in Obwalden and Nidwalden in December 1847, followed by those in Zug in February 1848, closely followed by those from Luzern, Freiburg and Uri. The last to go home were those occupying Wallis in April 1848. After that the only troops still mobilised were the Federal Staff. The Confederate government set up several military courts to deal with cases of indiscipline and desertions. Several hundred men, mostly Catholics, had refused the call-up and were sentenced to a few months' imprisonment. The Sonderbund troops were freely released back to their homes.

As the architect of the victory of the Confederation Dufour was awarded a sword of honour and 40,000 Swiss francs. The government of Geneva sent him and his immediate staff a large trout as a New Year's Day gift! Other marks of honour were refused. His duties at an end, his rank of general was rescinded and he returned to his home without an escort and without recognition. However, many people wanted an image of the victorious general – the only full-length portrait available had been painted in 1834. Prints and drawings were made from this picture, which, by a strange turn of fate, had been painted by Franz von Elgger, who had served in the Sonderbund army as chief of staff!

10

The Peace

Dufour had conducted a masterful campaign and had carried out the Confederate Diet's instructions to dissolve the Sonderbund in just three weeks. His intention of carrying out his instructions with minimum loss of life and with as little damage to property as possible had been completely successful. There had been some men killed and wounded and some houses had been looted or damaged, it is true, but it had been on a very small scale. The horrors of civil war had been avoided by the swiftness of the campaign and by Dufour's repeated orders to officers and soldiers to treat the 'enemy' with respect and forbearance.

As the situation deteriorated before the outbreak of hostilities, the governments of several European powers suggested a conference to settle the religious and political differences between the cantons. One suggestion was to refer the question of the role of the Jesuits to the Pope and the possible division of the Swiss cantons into two separate confederations, or even the break up of Switzerland altogether, with France and Austria taking over large parts of the country. As the powers considered the various options and prepared a document to present to the Swiss Diet, the Swiss themselves quickly opened the military campaign and just as quickly ended it. When the proposals were at last

Officers from the Confederate Brigade Frei at the Abbey of St Urbain in January 1848. (Steinhäuslin, *Bilder aus dem Sonderbundskriege im November 1847*, 1848)

Confederate troops enter Freiburg. (*Illustrated London News*)

Confederate troops returning home, January 1848. (Steinhäuslin, *Bilder aus dem Sonderbundskriege im November 1847*, 1848)

presented, the Swiss made no comment and when pressed for a response, replied that none was required as the situation had now been resolved! If France and Austria had taken military action, it may have ended as a full-scale European war.

The defeated cantons were forced to change their ruling councils to accept the views of the majority and to pay for the costs of the campaign, but there was no witch-hunt against individuals. The Jesuits were banned from the country and only allowed back in 1973. The new Constitution of 1848 established a Federal Swiss state that carefully balanced the authority of the central government with the rights retained by the cantons. This constitution, with revisions, remains to this day and has provided the country with stability and peace. Over the years, following the establishment of the new state, the money, weights and measures and postal service were standardised. The system of universal military service was retained until recently.

11

Uniforms of the Swiss Canton armies

The regiments raised by the Swiss government in support of Napoleon were clothed in red, a colour traditionally used by Swiss troops in foreign service. Prior to French intervention the cantons had used a variety of colours for their own armies and with the re-formation of the Swiss Confederation there was some return to this system. However, after 1817 agreement was reached amongst the cantons that the fusiliers and chasseurs in the infantry companies would wear blue with red facings, the rifle companies green with black facings, the artillery blue with red facings and cavalry, green with red facings.

This sounded simple in theory, but each canton interpreted the agreement in its own way. For example, Luzern published regulations in 1828 which specified a single-breasted dark blue tail coat for the fusiliers, with red collars and turnbacks to the tails of the coat, red piping down the front of the coat, around the cuffs and along the edges of the false pockets. The buttons were white metal. Trousers were white. In undress a French style 'bonnet de police' was worn with red piping and blue tassel. The French-style bell-topped shako had a blue pompon and white metal chinscales. No decoration was worn. The chasseur companies had the same pattern, the only difference was that the collar was yellow and that the forage cap was piped yellow with a yellow tassel. The shako carried a white metal hunting horn plate.

The Luzern rifle companies wore a green double-breasted coat and green trousers, with a black collar and yellow metal buttons to the coat. The forage cap was green with a green tassel and a yellow hunting horn badge. This badge was also worn in yellow metal

A typical officer's gorget. (Author's collection)

Infantry, dragoon and artillery campaign uniforms of troops from canton St Gallen, Confederate army. (Author's collection)

on the front of the shako. In 1829 the riflemen were given black cuffs and turnbacks to their coats. The artillery companies had a dark blue double-breasted coat with red turnbacks and red piping to the collar, cuffs, false pockets and on the front of the coat, with blue trousers. The shako had a yellow metal grenade plate and a red pompon. The forage cap was blue with red piping and tassel.

The cavalry had, at first, a blue single-breasted coat with red collar and turnbacks and piping to the cuffs and down the front of the coat. Later the basic blue was changed to green, with green booted overalls. Headgear was a shako with a blue pompon.

Other cantons wore variations of this uniform, but with differences in the detail. The Aargau fusiliers had a similar uniform, with red cuff flaps, blue fringeless epaulettes with red moons. The red turnbacks had blue star decorations. The 1st chasseur company in each battalion had green-fringed epaulettes with red moons and the 2nd chasseur company, green epaulette straps and fringes and yellow moons. All the chasseurs had a hunting horn badge on the turnbacks. Companies were distinguished by the pompons worn on the shako, 1st company, red ball and tuft; 2nd company, black ball and red tuft;

3rd company, yellow ball and red tuft; 4th company, blue ball and red tuft. Officers had a silver ball and red tuft. The 1st chasseur company had a green over red ball and red tuft and the 2nd chasseur company a green over yellow ball with a red tuft. The shako had yellow metal chinscales and plate and a canton cockade (see Chapter 4) secured by a yellow metal loop and button. All troops wore a mid-grey double-breasted greatcoat with a blue collar. Officers wore a plain blue double-breasted frock coat with silver buttons and a silver epaulette and contre-epaulette. In the field officers wore a silver gorget and white gloves.

The rifle companies of Aargau had a green single-breasted tail coat with black collar and turnbacks, green round cuffs, piped black with black cuff patches, yellow metal buttons. The epaulette straps and fringes were black with green moons, and green hunting horn decoration to the turnbacks. Trousers were green with black stripes along the outer seam, black gaiters and black shoes. The cylindrical black felt shako had a leather top and bottom band and peak, yellow metal chinscales, hunting horn plate and loop to hold the cockade, and a black ball with a green tuft.

The Aargau artillery uniform was a blue double-breasted tail coat, with red collar, piping round the cuffs and red cuff patches and short turnbacks, red fringed epaulettes and yellow metal buttons. The turnbacks had a blue grenade decoration. Trousers were blue piped red. There was a conical black shako with black leather chinstrap, but with yellow metal chinscales hooked up behind the red ball and tuft pompon. The shako plate consisted of crossed canons in yellow metal. Officers had long tails to the coat and a gold epaulette and contre-epaulette and grenade badges to the turnbacks. They wore a gold band round the top of the shako and in the field wore black gloves. Trousers had a broad red stripe either side of the outer seam.

The Waadt rifle companies had a green double-breasted tail coat with green collar, cuffs and turnbacks piped yellow, with yellow piping to the front of the coat and on the false pockets, yellow metal buttons on the coat and three further buttons at the back seam of the cuffs. Epaulettes had green straps and fringes and yellow moons. The turnbacks had a grenade decoration on the two outer flaps and a hunting horn on the inner flaps, all in yellow. The field cap was green with yellow piping and a mixed yellow/green tassel. The green trousers had a broad yellow stripe either side of the seam.The shako had yellow metal chinscales and an ornate plate bearing the canton coat of arms over an 'Amazon' shield. The pompon was green over yellow.

A contemporary painting by Emil Rittmeyer of canton St Gallen, depicting his four brothers setting out on campaign, shows a fusilier in greatcoat with a conical shako in a waterproof cover and rolled up trousers, a second fusilier wearing a conical shako with the greatcoat worn rolled across the body, an artilleryman with bell-topped shako and also a dragoon with a similar headdress.

In all cantons, the fusilier and chasseur companies had white belts and straps and the rifle companies, black.

The Battle of Gislikon was fought, in the main, between the troops of Luzern, described above and the regular troops of Zurich. These wore a similar uniform to other cantons – the fusilier companies were clothed in blue single-breasted tail coats with red collars, turnbacks and cuff patches and piping down the front of the coat, with blue trousers with red piping. Most of the Zurich troops wore the conical shako, introduced in 1843. It was in black felt with leather top and a leather bottom band and

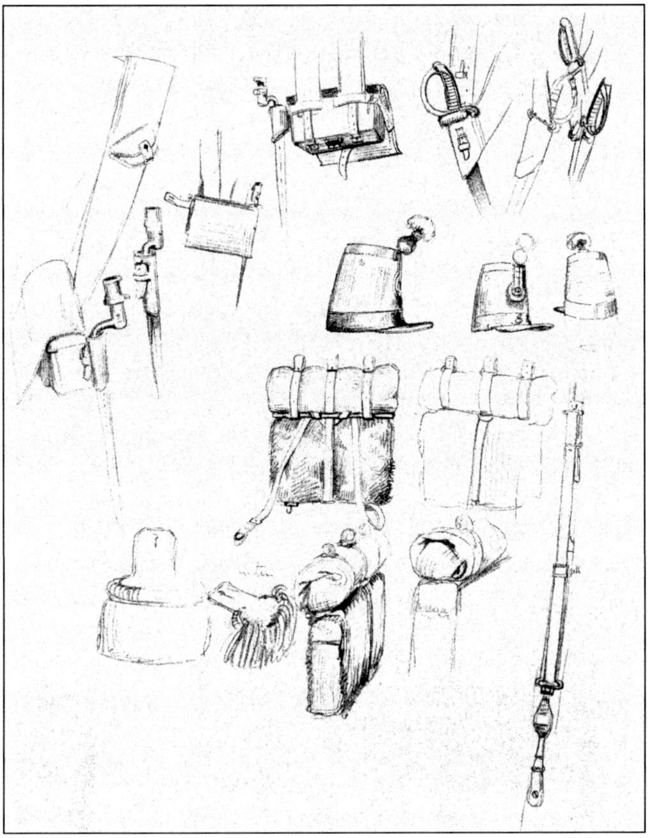

Close-up views of infantry uniforms and equipment. (Author's collection)

peak and chin strap. On the front of the shako, on the bottom band was a yellow metal numeral denoting the battalion number. Above that there was a large canton cockade of diagonally divided blue and white, held by a yellow metal strap and button. Over that was located a company coloured double pompon. Blue shoulder straps were piped red for the fusiliers and green-fringed epaulettes bore red moons for the chasseur companies. On campaign most troops wore a blue-grey greatcoat. Company officers wore a blue frock coat with silver buttons and a silver gorget, and an epaulette on the left shoulder and a contre-epaulette on the right.

The Zurich contingent included three cavalry companies. They were dressed in dark green tail coats and trousers with red collars, turnbacks cuff flaps and piping. The single-breasted coat was closed by a row of yellow metal buttons and the shoulders were protected by yellow metal scale epaulettes with red cloth backing. The trousers had a red stripe either side of the seam. They wore a black leather helmet, similar to contemporary Bavarian models, with yellow metal edging to the peak and chinscales and bands stiffening the crown. This bore a black fur crest. Troopers wore white gauntlets.

A uniform in the Swiss National Museum belonged to Doctor Kleinert, who was with Battalion Ginsberg No.9 at the Battle of Gisikon. He wore a mid-blue double-breasted tail coat with black collar, round cuffs and turnbacks. The collar was edged gold and had three gold lace bars on each side. The coat was worn open at the front to reveal a black lining to the lapels, and had two rows of gold buttons. The trousers are shown as white, but in the field it is likely that blue piped red trousers were worn. Headgear was a black bicorne with a gold loop holding a Zurich cockade. The doctor carried an officers' sword with gold fittings in a black leather scabbard. On the left arm was the ubiquitous red armband with a small white cross.

Contemporary pictures depicting troops in action show units wearing French Napoleonic, cylindrical and conical shakos and also forage caps. There are even some, un-named, units with Russian-style kiwer shakos! The only thing common to all Confederate troops was the Swiss brassard in red with a white cross, worn on the upper left arm. This was carried by all ranks from the commanding general down to private soldiers.

Every formation higher than the battalion was commanded by 'staff officers', supported by other officers, not connected to individual companies or battalions. In orders of battle they are referred to as 'Federal colonel' and were regular soldiers. Battalion commanders, if colonels, were employed by the cantons and, like private soldiers, were called out when needed. In the Confederation 'staff officers' wore a double-breasted long tail coat of dark green with red collar, turnbacks and cuffs with gold buttons and gold epaulettes. Headgear was a black bicorne with gold tassels and black feathers. The exception was General Dufour, who wore a bicorne with white feathers. Field dress was a dark green frock coat with black collar and cuffs and gold epaulettes, and dark green trousers with a red stripe either side of the seam. Senior officers wore a white sash with red stripes and the ubiquitous Federal armband of red with a white cross. Adjutants wore a white armband with red stripes.

Badges of rank for NCOs were similar to the contemporary French styles of diagonal stripes above the cuffs. Company officers had a silver-fringed epaulette on the left shoulder and a contre-epaulette on the right, and a silver pompon on the shako instead of the company colour. Battalion officers had a fringed epaulette on each shoulder. Officers wore a silver gorget, embossed with the canton coat of arms.

12

Canton cockades

All cantons were identified by a cockade worn on the shako just below the pompon. They were based on the heraldic colours associated with the flag of the canton and were in the form of coloured metal discs.

Confederates:

Zurich	Blue and white divided diagonally
Bern	Black, edged orange
Glarus	Red centre, then thin black, white and red outer
Solothurn	Red, edged white
Basel-land	Red, edged white
Schaffhausen	Black, edged green
Appenzell (outer)	Black, edged white
St. Gallen	Green, edged white
Graubunden	Blue centre, white edged blue
Aargau	Black, edged blue
Thurgau	Green and white divided diagonally
Tessin	Blue and red divided horizontally
Waadt	Green edged white
Geneva	Red edged yellow
Basel-Stadt	Black edged white

Sonderbund

Luzern	Blue and white divided horizontally
Uri	Black edged yellow
Schwyz	Red
Unterwalden- made up of two half cantons:	
Obwalden	White edged red
Nidwalden	Red edged white
Zug	Blue and white, alternate quarters (white upper and lower quarters)
Freiburg	White centre, black, white
Wallis	White edged red

Neutrals

Appenzell (Inner)	Small black centre with wide white outer
Neuenburg	Green centre, white edged red
Basel Land	Red, edged white

13

Swiss Battle Flags

The Swiss had no national flag before the French domination in 1798. Before that time, as regiments were raised within the Swiss borders and beyond raised in the pay of foreign powers, they adopted coloured flags based on the canton coat of arms. The regiments raised for French service carried a red and green standard with a representation of William Tell. When these troops returned home in 1815 they were presented with an honorary flag of a red field containing a white cross, which did not extend to the edge of the sheet. On the vertical arms of the cross was a sword wrapped in a laurel vine and on the horizontal arms the letters, in gold, FÜR VATERLAND || UND EHRE. On the reverse the letters were SCHWEIZERISCHE || EIDGENOSSCHENSCHAFT.

After 1803, with the re-founding of the Swiss confederation by Napoleon, individual cantons adopted flags bearing a white cross extending to the edges of the field and in the four quarters an arrangement of two colours in a flame pattern. Below the spearhead was fixed a cravat in red and white (the Swiss national colours).

In 1817 the colours of the flames in the quarters were, by canton:

Uri	yellow and black
Schwyz	all red, sometimes with a small white cross in the quarter near the hoist
Unterwalden	red and white
Luzern	white and blue
Zurich	blue and white
Glarus	red/black/white/red
Zug	white/blue/white
Bern	red and black
Freibourg	black and white
Solothurn	red and white
Basel Stadt	white and black
Basel Land,	white and red
Schaffhausen	green and black
Appenzell	white and black
St Gallen	green and white
Graubunden	black/white/blue
Aargau	black and blue
Thurgau	green and white
Tessin	red and blue quarters, no flames
Waadt	white and green
Wallis	white and red
Neuenburg	red and yellow

Geneva	yellow and red

In pre-Revolutionary times many of the flags had borne a heraldic emblem in the centre of the arms of the cross. This was now replaced, in most cases, by the canton name in gold letters.

A recommendation was made in the early 1830s that all cantons adopt a Confederation, or Federal flag of red with a white cross, similar to the 1815 honorary flag, but with the canton name on the horizontal white arm. It was first adopted by Aargau in 1833 and followed by others until, by 1840, all cantons carried the new flag. The red and white cravat was replaced by one in the canton colours from the list shown above. The sheet was made of silk four feet five inches square (1.3 metres).

Illustrations of the war show the Confederate battalions carrying the Federal flag in battle. It is likely that the Sonderbund cantons still carried their former colours, especially the Landwehr units. The last use of the old style 'flame' flags was in 1865, when they were finally replaced by the modern Federal flag.

14

Some Swiss commanders

Dufour

William-Henry Dufour was selected by the Confederate government to the command of the Federal forces against the Sonderbund. Aged 60 in 1847, he had had a varied career since his birth in the German town of Konstanz in 1787. His parents had moved there to escape unrest in their home town of Geneva (Genf). Two years later the family returned to Geneva, where Dufour attended the local schools. His father was involved in local politics and had sat in the National Assembly of Geneva. In 1807, when Geneva was part of the French Empire, he moved to Paris and studied in the École Polytechnique, the premier science school in France. In 1809 he continued his studies at the engineer school in Metz. As an engineer officer he entered the French army and took part in several campaigns. On Napoleon's escape from Elba he was given command of Fort l'Écluse, which commanded the access to the Rhône valley from Switzerland. He defended the fort against the Austrian general Frimont. In 1817, now a captain, he retuned to Geneva and was employed as an engineer, showing particular skill as a builder of bridges.

Dufour continued his career in the Swiss army and was promoted to lieutenant-colonel in 1820 and full colonel in 1827, the highest rank in the Swiss army. In 1831 he was appointed Chief of the General Staff. In this capacity he chaired a commission to make a new map of Switzerland, which was eventually completed in 1864. He also championed the adoption of the Swiss Confederation flag to be carried by all battalions of the cantons.

In 1822 Dufour began writing books on military topics, one of which caught the attention of the Emperor of Russia, who offered him the rank of major-general in his army. In 1835 he met Louis Napoleon, who was then living in exile in Switzerland. Louis Napoleon's name appears on a book on engineering, but it is supposed that Dufour was the real author.

When it became apparent, late in 1847, that war would break out with the Sonderbund, the Confederation government approached Dufour to take command of the army. His appointment was confirmed on 21 October, not without some behind the scenes politicking from a rival candidate. He was given the temporary rank of general for the duration of the conflict, which ended with the surrender of the canton of Wallis on 1 December. In September 1848, with a revolutionary war just over the border in Baden, he was again given command of the Federal army, then again in 1856 when a conflict with Prussia threatened over the future of the canton of Neuenburg. His last command was in 1859, when war broke out between France, Italy and Austria and threatened to spill over the Swiss southern border.

Dufour took part in Swiss politics, firstly in Geneva, and later in the national parliament. In 1863 he joined Henri Dunant in what would eventually become the Red Cross and was its first chairman in 1863-1864. Dufour died in Geneva on 14 July 1875.

Gmür

Dominik Gmür was born in 1800 and studied languages and mathematics in Milan. He entered politics in 1831 as a Radical in the government of Canton St Gallen. It was through his influence that the district voted against the Sonderbund in 1847. He was appointed a Federal Colonel in 1839, which rank he retained until 1854. He was victor in the fight at Meierskappel and later accepted the surrender of canton Schwyz to the Confederation.

Kalbermatten

Although descended from a distinguished Swiss family, Baron Wilhelm Theodor von Kalbermatten was born in the Netherlands in 1793, where his father was a captain in the Dutch army. In 1804 he joined the Spanish service as a cadet in the Regiment de Courten and in 1809 he was promoted to lieutenant in the Rifle corps of Castile. At the first restoration in France in 1814 he, along with his father and brother, joined the 4th Swiss Regiment. He later moved to the 3rd Battalion of the 8th Swiss Regiment of the French Royal Guards, where he served until the 1830 revolution, when the Swiss troops were dismissed. He entered politics in canton Wallis as a conservative and became leader of the canton forces. After the war he travelled to Rome where he became a general officer in the Papal army until its disbandment in 1870. He stayed on in Rome, where he died in 1875.

Maillardoz

François Philippe de Maillardoz, 3rd Marquess of Maillardoz of Rue was born on 6 September 1783 in Freiburg and died on 6 June 1853 in Luzern. He enlisted in the armies of the French First Empire in 1806 where he participated in the campaigns against Prussia and Austria with the rank of captain. He was awarded the Legion of Honour after the Battle of Eylau.

After the restoration in France, he joined the Swiss Guard of the King of France, with the rank of lieutenant-colonel, and in this position, defended Paris for Charles X during the 1830 revolution. In parallel, he pursued a political career in the canton of Freiburg.

Back in Switzerland in 1831, he was appointed prefect and colonel of the Federal Army. Between 1836 and 1842, he was a councillor of state, supporting the Conservatives. He was appointed a Commander of the Legion of Honour by Louis-Philippe in 1841.

In 1847 he was made inspector general of the Freiburg militia. One of the contenders for the title of Commander of the Army of the Sonderbund, Salis-Soglio was chosen instead, Maillardoz preferring to command the Freiburg division during the war. Following the surrender of Freiburg, Maillardoz was falsely accused of treason. He fled to Neuenburg and Besançon, and thence to Luzern where he published, in 1850, his memoirs of his participation in the events of Freiburg in 1847.

Rillet-Constant

Frederick Louis Jacques Rillet Constant was commander of the Federal First Division and was born in 1794. In 1812 served as a lieutenant in a French cuirassier regiment and fought in the battles of Lützen, Bautzen, Leipzig and Hanau. He remained in France after the fall of Napoleon and commanded a company of Guards before he returned to Geneva in 1832. As with other men of this time he was also a politician, active in the government of Geneva. In 1837 he was appointed a colonel on the Federal Staff. After the Sonderbund War he remained in the Federal army and in 1852 was appointed inspector of cavalry. He retained this post until his death in 1856.

Salis-Soglio

The man appointed by the Sonderbund to command its armies was Johan Ulrich von Salis-Soglio. Of Protestant aristocratic background, he was a conservative politically, but sympathised with the Catholic cantons. His appointment was announced on 11 December 1845 with the rank of general. He was born in 1790 and entered the Swiss military at the age of 19. In 1811 he was a junior officer in the General Staff of the army. In 1812 he joined the Bavarian army and fought in the campaigns of 1813 and 1814, being present at several actions including the battles of Hanau, Bar-sur-Aube and Arcis-sur-Aube. In 1815 he left Switzerland for the Netherlands were he joined one of the Swiss regiments in Dutch service. He changed to a cuirassier regiment, becoming its colonel in 1828 and by 1839 had been promoted to major-general. In that year he returned to Switzerland and two years later became a colonel on the General Staff. He resigned in 1844. He led the Luzern forces in person at Gislikon and was wounded in the head by a splinter from a cannon ball. After the surrender of the Sonderbund he escaped into Lombardy and retired into private life. He died in 1874.

Schwarzenberg

Prince Friedrich Karl Johann Nepomuk Joseph zu Schwarzenberg was the son and heir of the princely house of that name, and held the rank of major-general in the Austrian army. He was born in Vienna in 1799. He had already visited Luzern before the outbreak of hostilities and was well favoured by many Sonderbund leaders. He was considered for the chief command, but for political reasons could not accept. He nevertheless took on the role of adjutant-general to Salis-Soglio with special responsibility for organising the militia. When asked by fellow officers in Milan (capital of Austrian Lombardy) what he needed for his appointment, he replied, "Just my sword." He tried to organise a defence of Freiburg by the militia, but events moved too fast. After the surrender of Luzern, he managed to return to Milan, not without difficulty.

Sonnenberg

One of the senior officers to be considered for the command of the Sonderbund army, Ludwig von Sonnenberg was born in Luzern in 1782 of an old Catholic and aristocratic family. He joined the army of the Helvetic Republic at the age of 19 and two years later, in 1803, moved to the French army and fought in Spain. He was taken prisoner by the Spaniards in 1808 and later handed over to the British where he remained until 1812. He returned to Switzerland in 1814 and was appointed commander of the Federal forces in Geneva. In 1824 he took service in the kingdom of Naples and rose to the rank of general. In 1845 he became a Luzern State Councillor and inspector of militia. He chose not to flee the county after the defeat of the Sonderbund and was imprisoned for several months. He died in 1850.

Ziegler

The man who contributed most to the Federal victory at Gislikon was one of Dufour's divisional commanders, Colonel Paul Charles Edward Ziegler. He was from the town of Zurich and his father was an army officer who fought against Napoleon. He was born in 1800 and at the age of 15 joined his father's regiment in Dutch service. By 1829 he had become the battalion adjutant, when he resigned his commission and returned to Switzerland. In Zurich he was appointed lieutenant-colonel and commander of a Zurich battalion. He was active in local politics and between 1837 and 1840 was elected mayor. In 1844 he became a colonel in the General Staff and was chosen by Dufour as commander of the Confederate Fourth Division. He later became Chief of Staff and was active in politics, representing Zurich in the national parliament from 1860 to 1866. He lived in Zurich until his death in 1882.

Appendix I

Strength and Organisation of the Confederation Army, November 1847

Commander in Chief	General W. H. Dufour
Chief of Staff	Colonel Frei-Hérosé
General-Adjutant	Colonel Zimmerli
Artillery commander	Colonel von Drelli
Quartermaster	Colonel Buchwalder
Engineer commander	Lieutenant-Colonel Gatschet
Cavalry commander	Lieutenant-Colonel von Linden
Senior War commissioner	Colonel Abys
Senior Medical officer	Doctor Flügel

First Division
Colonel Rilliet-Constant, headquarters at Lausanne
Division staff – 41 and 38 musicians
Brigadiers – Colonels Bundi, Kurz, Veillon and Nicollier

Troops drawn from the cantons of Waadt and Geneva:

	Elite	Reserve	Total
Infantry companies	72	29	101
Rifle companies	10	3	13
Cavalry companies	3	1	4
Artillery batteries	5	1	6
Engineer companies	1	1	2

Strength:

	Men	Horses
Elite	10,032	891
Reserve	3,767	303
Total	13,799	1194

Second Division

Colonel Burkhardt, headquarters at Basel
Brigadiers – Colonels, Frey, Bontems and Bourgeois

Troops drawn from the cantons Bern, Solothurn and Basel-Land:

	Elite	Reserve	Total
Infantry companies	74	60	134
Rifle companies	5	6	11
Cavalry companies	3	2½	5½
Artillery batteries	5	4½	9½
Engineer companies	1	1	2

Strength:

	Men	Horses
Elite	10,490	798
Reserve	8,466	633
Total	18,956	1431

Third Division

Colonel von Donats, headquarters at Solothurn
Division staff – 16 and 34 musicians
Brigadiers – Colonels Gerwer, Hauser and Marca

Troops drawn from cantons Bern, Aargau, Solothurn and Basel-Land:

	Elite	Reserve	Total
Infantry companies	42	7	49
Rifle companies	5	-	5
Cavalry companies	2	-	3
Artillery batteries	3	-	3
Engineer companies	1	-	1

Strength:

	Men	Horses
Elite	6,078	520
Reserve	898	15
Total	6,976	535

Fourth Division

Colonel Ziegler, headquarters at Aarau
Division staff – 16 and 30 musicians
Brigadiers – Colonels Egloff, König and Müller

Troops drawn from cantons Zurich, Aargau, St Gallen, Thurgau, Appenzell (Outer) and one unit each from Solothurn, Glarus and Graubunden:

	Elite	Reserve	Total
Infantry companies	66	36	102
Rifle companies	6	2	8
Cavalry companies	2	-	2
Artillery batteries	3	2	5
Engineer companies	1	-	1

Strength:

	Men	Horses
Elite	8,700	564
Reserve	4,411	129
Total	13,111	693

Fifth Division

Colonel Gmür, headquarters at Zurich
Brigadiers – Colonels Blumer, Isler and Ritter

Troops drawn from cantons Zurich, St Gallen, Thurgau, Schaffhausen, Glarus and Appenzell (Outer):

	Elite	Reserve	Total
Infantry companies	66	78	144
Rifle companies	5	7	12
Cavalry companies	2	½	2½
Artillery batteries	3	-	3
Engineer companies	1	-	1

Strength:

	Men	Horses
Elite	8,160	559
Reserve	9,630	177
Total	17,790	727

Sixth Division

Colonel Luvini, headquarters at Tessin
Brigadiers – Colonels Pioda and Eduard von Salis-Soglio (younger brother of the Sonderbund army commanding general)

Troups drawn from cantons Tessin and Graubunden:

	Elite	Reserve	Total
Infantry companies	36	-	36
Rifle companies	4	-	4
Cavalry companies	-	-	0
Artillery batteries	-	1	1
Engineer companies	-	-	0

Strength:

	Men	Horses
Elite	5,148	70
Reserve	122	78
Total	5,270	148

Cavalry Reserve

Lieutenant-Colonel von Linden
Brigadiers – Majors Rieter, Ott and Karlen
Strength – nine cavalry companies from cantons Zurich, Bern, Aargau, St Gallen, Thurgau and Basel-Land: 576 men and 594 horses.

Artillery reserve

Lieutenant-Colonel Denzler
6 batteries with 938 men and 767 horses

Strength of the army:

	Elite	Reserve	Total
Infantry companies	350	210	560
Rifle companies	35	18	53
Cavalry companies	21	4	25
Artillery batteries	25	8½	33½
Engineer companies	5	2	7

Strength:

	Men	Horses
Elite	50,122	4,754
Reserve	27,294	1,335
Total	77,416	6,089

As so many men came forward above the regulation strengths, the actual total came to 89,906 men.

In addition, further reserve formations were commissioned. In support of the Second Division the Bernese Reserve Division was mobilised under the command of Colonel Ochsenbein. It had four brigades, the brigadiers were: First Brigade – Colonel Knechtenhofer, Second Brigade – Piquerez; Third Brigade – Walthard; Fourth Brigade – Chissele. It had a total strength of 9,544 men. In support of the Fourth Division was the Aargau Landwehr Division under Colonel Rothpletz, and supporting the Fifth Division were the Zurich Landwehr, to which the Landwehr of Thurgau, Glarus and Appenzell (Outer) were added, commanded by Lieutenant-Colonel Schulhes.

Appendix II

Confederate cantons' numbers of Elite, Reserve and Landwehr formations, November 1847

Canton	Infantry battalions	Rifle companies	Cavalry companies	Artillery companies
Zurich	20	8	3	9
Bern	56	18	10	20
Glarus	3	5	-	1
Solothurn	3	-	1	2
Basel-Land	3	3	2	2
Schaffhausen	2	-	1	-
Appenzell	4	4	-	-
St Gallen	8	3	3	4
Graubunden	6	6	-	-
Aargau	24	6	3	6
Thurgau	6	3	2	-
Tessin	4	5	-	2
Waadt	48	12	5	13
Geneva	6	1	1	4
Basel-Stadt	2½	1	-	4
Totals	195½	75	31	89[1]

1 The cumulative figure of the subtotals produces a figure of only 67 artillery companies – this numeric discrepancy is a result of printed sources containing apparent inconsistencies and contradictions.

Appendix III

Strength of Confederate Cantons, November 1847

Canton	Men	Guns
Zurich	13,075	28
Bern	23,247	54
Glarus	2,238	5
Solothurn	2,434	4
Basel-Stadt	540	4
Basel-Land	2,052	-
Schaffhausen	1,332	-
Appenzell (Outer)	1,889	-
St Gallen	6,458	12
Graubunden	3,849	-
Aargau	12,533	25
Thurgau	4,076	-
Tessin	3,418	4
Waadt	19,198	32
Wallis	226	-
Geneva	2,284	4
Others	13	-
Totals	98,862	172

Appendix IV

Organisation of the Sonderbund Army

Commander in Chief	General Johan Ulrich von Salis-Solgio
Chief of Staff	Colonel von Elgger
General Adjutant	Lieutenant-Colonel Vinzenz Müller
Engineer officer	Lieutenant-Colonel Emanuel Müller
Artillery commander	Lieutenant-Colonel Göldlin

1st Division

Colonel Rüttimann
Brigadiers – Colonels Kost, Zur Eilgen and Ulrich Schmid
Commander of the Luzern Landwehr – Colonel Pasqual Tschudi
Brigadiers – Majors Plazid Segesser and Zeeleder von Steinegg

2nd Division

Colonel Theodor Ab-Yberg
Brigadiers – Captains Schmid and Letter
Commander of the Landsturm of canton Schwyz – Lieutenant-Colonel Dominik Ab-Yberg

Freiburg Division

Colonel Maillardoz
Brigadiers – Lieutenant-Colonels Schaller, Albiez and Moret

Wallis Division

General Wilhelm von Kalbermatten
Chief of Staff – Colonel Louis von Courten
Brigadiers – Colonels Tassiner, von Cocatrir and Adrian von Courten
Staff chaplain – Chorherr de Rivaz

Appendix V

Sonderbund Cantons' Strengths (including Landwehr)

Canton	Infantry battalions	Rifle companies	Cavalry companies	Artillery companies
Luzern	12	8	1	5
Uri	2	4	-	2
Schwyz	8	8	-	2
Unterwalden	4	8	-	2
Zug	2	4	-	1
The two cantons below were physically split from the central Sonderbund cantons and their armies remained within their own borders:				
Freiburg	8	4	1½	4
Wallis	6	4	-	4
Totals	42	40	2½	20

Appendix VI

Sonderbund Army Order of Battle for Gisikon and Meierskappel, 23 November 1847

Commander: General Salis-Soglio

GISIKON
1st Division (troops of canton Luzern)
Colonel Rüttimann

1st Brigade
Colonel Zurgilgen

Elite Battalion	No. 4	X. Schmid	721 men
Landwehr Battalion	No. 6	Fehlmann	614 men
Landwehr Battalion	No. 8	Göldlin	647 men
Elite Rifle Company	No. 1	Hurter	161 men
Landwehr Rifle Coy	No. 1	Willmann	131 men
Landwehr Rifle Coy	No. 2	Meier	101 men

Brigade total – 2,375 men

2nd Brigade
Lieutenant-Colonel Kost

Elite Battalion	No. 2	Schobinger	677 men
Landwehr Battalion	No. 4	Zemp	465 men
Landwehr Battalion	No. 5	Schiffmann	567 men
Elite Rifle Coy	No. 2	Hartmann	160 men
Landwehr Rifle Coy	No. 2	Schlapfer	103 men

Brigade total – 1,972 men

3rd Brigade
Lieutenant-Colonel J.-U. Schmid

Elite Battalion	No. 1	Ed. Segesser	748 men
Elite Battalion	No. 3	Meier-Bielmann	701 men
Landwehr Battalion	No. 7	Weingartner	580 men
Elite Rifle coy	No. 3	Segesser	152 men
Landwehr Rifle coy	No. 3	Hurter	159 men

Brigade total – 2,340 men

Artillery

Artillery Company	Pfyffer	4 guns	90 men
Artillery Company	Nager	4 guns	83 men

Artillery total – 8 guns, 173 men

Division total – 7,858 men and 8 guns[1]

MEIERSKAPPEL
2nd Division
Colonel Ab-Yberg

1st Brigade

(ex-) Federal Colonel François-Charles Letter

Elite Battalion	Hediger from Schwyz	538 men
Elite Battalion	Reding from Schwyz	537 men
Landwehr Battalion	Müller from Schwyz	537 men
Landwehr Battalion	Dober from Schwyz	536 men
Elite Battalion	Moos from Zug	681 men
Landwehr Battalion	Andermatt from Zug	649 men
4 Rifle companies from Schwyz		412 men
2 Rifle companies from Zug		200 men

Brigade total – 4,090 men

2nd Brigade

Colonel Schmid

Battalion Jauch from Uri	503 men
Battalion Rothlin from Obwalden	418 men
Battalion Wursch from Nidwalden	440 men
Battalion Courten from Wallis	600 men
2 Rifle companies from Uri	237 men
2 Rifle companies from Obwalden	200 men
2 Rifle companies from Nidwalden	200 men

Brigade total – 2,598 men

Artillery

Artillery Company	Hegner from Schwyz	4 guns
Artillery Company	Ulrich from Schwyz	4 howitzers
Artillery Company	Ulrich from Zug	3 guns

Artillery total – 11 guns, number of men unknown

1 The cumulative figure of the subtotals produces a figure of only 6,860 men – this numeric discrepancy is a result of printed sources containing apparent inconsistencies and contradictions.

Division total – 6,906 men and 11 guns[2]

Army Artillery Reserve

Artillery Company	Mazzola from Luzern	4 guns
Artillery Company	Schwyzer from Luzern	4 guns
Artillery Company	von Moos from Luzern	4 guns
Artillery Company	Muheim from Uri	6 guns

Army Artillery Reserve total – 18 guns, number of men unknown

The Luzern armoury had a battery of Congreve rockets in the inventory, but there is no indication that they were brought out for use.

2 See footnote 1. The cumulative figure using the subtotals comes to 6,688 men and 11 guns. The discrepancy in this instance can probably be explained by adding on the men from the two artillery companies.

Appendix VII

Confederation Army Order of Battle for Gisikon and Meierskappel, 23 November 1847

Commander General Dufour

GISIKON
Fourth Division
Confederate Colonel Ziegler

1st Brigade
Confederate Colonel Egloff

Elite Battalion Ginsberg	No.9 from Zurich	828 men
Elite Battalion Benz	No.11 from Zurich	660 men
Elite Battalion Häusler	No.15 from Aargau	753 men
Elite Battalion Zuppinger	No.34 from Zurich	590 men
Rifle Coy Kries	No.26 from Thurgau	99 men
Rifle Coy Bleuler	No.35 from Zurich	118 men

Brigade total – 3,048 men

2nd Brigade
Confederate Colonel König

Elite Battalion Berner	No.42 from Aargau	722 men
Elite Battalion Fasi	No.48 from Zurich	721 men
Elite Battalion Ernst	No.49 from Thurgau	712 men
Elite Battalion Banzinger	No.66 from Appenzell	495 men
Rifle Coy Hanhart	No.5 from Thurgau	103 men
Rifle Coy Kuster	No.31 from St Gallen	109 men

Brigade total – 2,862 men

3rd Brigade
Confederate Colonel Müller

Elite Battalion Basler	No.64 from Zurich	819 men
Elite Battalion Martignoni	No.31 from St Gallen	790 men
Elite Battalion Kunzli	No.38 from Aargau	707 men
Rifle Coy Blumer	No.41 from Glarus	103 men
Rifle Coy Tscharner	No.16 from Graubunden	101 men

Brigade total – 2,520 men

Cavalry

Company Hanhart	No.3 from Zurich	46 men
Company Bally	No.8 from Solothurn	59 men

Cavalry total – 105 men

Artillery

6-pounder cannon Battery Rust No.9 from Solothurn	119 men
6-pounder cannon Battery Müller, No.10 from Aargau	172 men
12-pounder howitzer battery Schweizer, No.22 from Zurich	129 men

Artillery total – 420 men

Other units

½ Park Company	No.42 from St Gallen	58 men
Reserve Artillery Park		52 men
Sapper Company Jeuch	No.3 from Aargau	100 men
Ambulance Section	No.III and Extra-section No.VI	18 men

Subtotal – 228 men
Divison total – 9,183 men

First Reserve

Colonel Rothpletz

1st Brigade

Lieutenant-colonel Häusler

Battalion Tschudi	No.87 from Aargau	617 men
Battalion Oehlhafen	No.88 from Aargau	617 men
Battalion Diebold	No.101 from Aargau	549 men
Rifle Coy Ringier	No.47 from Aargau	141 men

Brigade total – 1,924 men

2nd Brigade

Lieutenant-colonel Schmitter

Battalion Ringier	No.89 from Aargau	575 men
Battalion Baldinger	No.102 from Aargau	578 men
Battalion Cellier	No.100 from Aargau	623 men
Rifle Coy Suter	No.48 from Aargau	95 men

Brigade total – 1,871 men

Cavalry

Company Hägler	from Basel-Land	41 men

Artillery

One 6-pounder battery, half-battery of 12-pounders and half-battery 24-pounder howitzers from Aargau and Battery No.32 from Basel-Land

Sapper company Hemmann	from Aargau	95 men

First Reserve total – 4,266 men

Second Reserve

Battalion Durr	from Aargau	344 men
Battalion Steiner	from Aargau	395 men
Battalion Halder	from Aargau	448 men
Battalion Metzger	from Aargau	718 men
Battalion Schmutziger	from Aargau	339 men
Battalion Ruetschi	from Aargau	466 men
Rifle Coy. Durr	from Aargau	38 men
Rifle Coy. Siebenmann	from Aargau	136 men
Rifle Coy. Halder	from Aargau	36 men
Rifle Coy. Buhler	from Basel-Land	66 men
Rifle Coy. GauMüller	from Basel-Land	67 men
Cavalry Coy. Halder	from Aargau	17 men
Cavalry Coy. Metzger	from Aargau	13 men

Artillery – three detachments with 83 men

Second Reserve total – 2,929 men[1]

MEIRESKAPPEL
Fifth Division

Confederate Colonel Gmür

1st Brigade

Colonel Blumer

Battalion Brunner	No.3 from Zurich	632 men
Battalion Meyer	No.29 from Zurich	568 men
Battalion Labhardt	No.7 from Thurgau	712 men
Rifle Coy Huber	No.21 from Zurich	102 men
Rifle Coy Kern	No.18 from Appenzell	100 men

Brigade total – 2,114 men

1 The cumulative figure of the subtotals produces a figure of 3,166 men – this numeric discrepancy is a result of printed sources containing apparent inconsistencies and contradictions.

2nd Brigade

Colonel Isler

Battalion Meyer	No.47 from Appenzell	497 men
Battalion Schmid	No.5 from Zurich	610 men
Battalion Hilti	No.63 from St Gallen	790 men
Rifle Coy Zeller	No.2 from Zurich	122 men
Rifle Coy Baumann	No.37 from St Gallen	125 men

Brigade total – 2,144 men

3rd Brigade

Colonel Ritter

Battalion Kappeler	No.14 from Thurgau	713 men
Battalion Schindler	No.73 from Glarus	641 men
Battalion Bernold	No.21 from St Gallen	790 men
Rifle Coy A.R. Banziger	No.20 from Appenzell	101 men
Rifle Coy Mölin	No.36 from Graubunder	88 men

Brigade total – 2,333 men

Cavalry

Company Caspar	No.1 from Schaffhausen	64 men
Company Metzmer	No.9 from St Gallen	64 men

Cavalry total – 128 men

Artillery

6-pounder cannon battery Scheller, No.1 from Zurich	123 men
6-pounder cannon battery Zeller, No.20 from Zurich	116 men
12-pounder howitzer battery Zollikofer from St Gallen	122 men

Artillery total – 361 men

Other troops

½ Park Company	No.42 from St Gallen	57 men
Reserve Artillery Park		30 men
Ambulance section		20 men

Subtotal – 107 men

Division total – 8,143 men[2]

Fifth Division Reserve

1st Brigade

Colonel Schulthetz

2 See footnote 1. In this instance, the cumulative figure from the subtotals comes to 7,187 men.

Battalion Bleuler	No.90 from Zurich	510 men
Battalion Schulthetz	No.91 from Zurich	569 men
Battalion Meyer	No.38 from Zurich	492 men
Battalion Haab	No 93 from Zurich	638 men
Rifle Coy Staub	No.54 from Zurich	114 men
Rifle Coy Schärer	No.55 from Zurich	100 men

Brigade total – 2,423 men

2nd Brigade
Colonel Bringolf

Battalion Bringolf	No.94 from Schaffhausen	366 men
Battalion Schnell	No.95 from St Gallen	790 men
Battalion Metzmer	No.96 from St Gallen	301 men
Rifle Coy Leuzinger	No.49 from Glarus	101 men
Rifle Coy Blumer	No.50 from Glarus	100 men

Brigade total – 1,658 men

3rd Brigade
Colonel Keller

Battalion Merkli	No.97 from Thurgau	701 men
Battalion Zellweger	No.98 from Appenzell	481 men
Battalion Blumer	No.99 from Glarus	643 men
Rifle Coy Ammann	No.53 from Thurgau	101 men
Rifle Coy Rohner	No.51 from Thurgau	81 men

Brigade total – 2,007 men

Cavalry

Company Reisser	from Thurgau	63 men
Company Sulzberger	from St Gallen	56 men

Cavalry total – 119 men

Artillery
Three 6-pounder batteries

Sapper Company Irminger	from Zurich	152 men

Fifth Division Reserve total – 6,792 men

Second line troops attached to the Fifth Division (not part of the above organisation)
4th Brigade
Federal Colonel Bernold

Battalion Treichler	from Zurich	485 men
Battalion Stahel	from Zurich	609 men

Battalion Schnell	from St Gallen	633 men
Rifle Company Bösch	from St Gallen	117 men
Rifle Company Langer	from Glarus	120 men

Brigade total – 1,964 men

5th Brigade
Colonel Fierz

Battalion Egg	from Zurich	804 men
Battalion Hablützel	from Zurich	633 men
Battalion Bühler	from Zurich	633 men
Rifle Company Bosshardt	from Zurich	99 men
Rifle Company Stapfer	from Zurich	84 men

Brigade total – 2,253 men

Total of unattached troops – 5,001 men[3]

3 See footnote 1. In this instance the cumulative figure from the subtotals comes to 4,217 men.

Appendix VIII

Elite Contingent Battalions

'Elite' battalion number	Canton
1	Bern
2	Tessin
3	Zurich
4	Aargau
5	Zurich
6	Neuenburg
7	Thurgau
8	Tessin
9	Zurich
10	Waadt
11	Zurich
12	Tessin
13	Luzern
14	Thurgau
15	Aargau
16	Bern
17	Aargau
18	Bern
19	Bern
20	Genf
21	St Gallen
22	Graubunden
23	Neuenburg
24	Luzern
25	Tessin
26	Waadt
27	Basel-Land
28	St Gallen
29	Zurich
30	Bern
31	St Gallen
32	Schwyz
33	Luzern
34	Zurich
35	Wallis
36	Bern
37	Bern
38	Aargau

39	Freiburg
40	Wallis
41	Aargau
42	Aargau
43	Bern
44	Solothurn
45	Waadt
46	Waadt
47	Appenzell (Outer)
48	Zurich
49	Thurgau
50	Waadt
51	Graubunden
52	St Gallen
53	Wallis
54	Bern
55	Bern
56	Freiburg
57	Luzern
58	Bern
59	Bern
60	Bern
61	Freiburg
62	Bern
63	St Gallen
64	Zurich
65	Graubunden
66	Luzern
67	Bern
68	St Gallen
69	Bern
70	Waadt
71	Schaffhausen
72	Solothurn
73	Glarus
74	Obwalden (3 companies), Nidwalden (2 companies)

Appendix IX

Rifle Companies

Rifle company number	Canton
1	Bern
2	Zurich
3	Waadt
4	Bern
5	Thurgau
6	Uri
7	Wallis
8	Waadt
9	Bern
10	Waadt
11	Nidwalden
12	Glarus
13	Freiburg
14	Neuenburg
15	Aargau
16	Graubunden
17	Neuenburg
18	Appenzell (Outer)
19	Basel-Land
20	Appenzell (Outer)
21	Zurich
22	Zurich
23	Schwyz
24	Obwalden
25	Freiburg
26	Thurgau
27	Bern
28	Zug
29	Bern
30	Waadt
31	St Gallen
32	Wallis
33	Bern
34	Luzern
35	Zurich
36	Graubunden
37	St Gallen
38	Aargau

39	Luzern
40	Aargau
41	Glarus
42	Schwyz
43	Luzern
44	Tessin
45	Tessin

Annotated Bibliography

As well as listing references used for this book, I have also added a few comments where necessary. The German *Fraktur* script referred to below is the Gothic style script used in many German language books until the 1930s. Although it can be hard to read at first, after a little practice it becomes quite readable. Books marked with an asterisk (*) can be viewed on the 'Google Books' site from the internet.

Anon., *The Cities of Europe, and theatre of war and revolution, in views, maps, and plans. With historical and descriptive letterpress**, London 1850. A travel book for English tourists. In two volumes, Volume 2 includes an account of the Swiss Civil war.

Anon., *Der Untergang des Sonderbundes und die Austreibung der Jesuiten durch die siegreiche eidgenössische Armee**, Bern 1848. A contemporary account of the war with organisation and strengths of both armies and casualty lists by canton and branch of service. German *Fraktur* script.

*Annual Register … of the year 1847**, London 1848. This publication covers the events of the year, both domestic and foreign, in considerable depth. It commenced publication in the mid-18th Century and each volume contains a mine of information, from world events, British parliamentary history to obituaries of eminent people and local news. The 1847 edition contains a chapter on Switzerland, not only events of the year, but also the background to the war.

Barnes, David, "The Battle of Gislikon", *The Foreign Correspondent* issue 32 (August 1996), the newsletter of the Continental Wars Society.

Bonaparte, Prince Napoleon-Louis, *Manuel d'Artillerie à l'usage des officiers d'artillerie de la République helvétique**, Zurich, Strasbourg and Paris, 1836. Possibly written by Louis Napoleon in his capacity as a captain of the canton Bern artillery, although William-Henry Dufour, later commander of the Confederate forces, may have been its actual author. Illustrated treatise including a section on Congreve rockets.

Burlet, Jürg, curator of uniforms and flags at the Swiss National Museum, Zurich. Correspondence with the author.

Butler, A. J., 'Gislikon' in *Battles of the Nineteenth Century* Volume 1, London, 1896. A 'popular' account from this Victorian-era series published by Cassell and Company. Butler provides a little background with a blow by blow of the major battle of the campaign.

Crétineau-Joly, J., *Histoire du Sonderbund*, Paris 1850. Good description of events of the war.

Dufour, G. H., *Allgemeiner Bericht des Eidgenössischen Oberbefehlshabers über die Bewaffnung und den Feldzug von 1847**, Bern and Zurich 1848. Dufour's own account of the campaign, includes his calculations of casualties on both sides. German *Fraktur* script.

Dufour, G. H. *Cours de tactique**, Paris and Geneva, 1840. As well as a practical engineer, Dufour was a well-read officer and applied his studies to a treatise on infantry tactics. Among his references are Xenophon, Frederick the Great and Prince Louis Napoleon Bonaparte. Includes the organisation of the Swiss forces as they existed in 1840. Dufour's book on tactics was also translated into Russian.

Elgger, Franz von, *Des Kantons Luzern und seiner Bundesgenossen Kampf gegen den Radikalismus vom 8. Dezember 1844 bis 24. November 1847 und mein Antheil an demselben**, Schaffhausen 1850. Written by the former Chief of Staff of the Sonderbund army, contains orders of battle, company strengths and casualty lists.

Heer, Albert & Binder, Gottlieb, *Der Sonderbund*, Zurich 1913. Account of the political and military campaign accompanied by 160 illustrations of contemporary cartoons, personalities, battle scenes and photographs of towns and villages where the action took place. Some maps, including a detailed plan of the battle of Gislikon with a Confederate order of battle. German *Fraktur* script.

Leuthy, Johann Jakob, *Récit des derniers événements survenus en Suisse, par suite de l'alliance séparée (Sonderbund), fondee le 14 septembre 1843, aux Bains de Rothen, entre les cantons de Lucerne, Uri, Schwyz, Unterwalden, Zug, Fribourg et Valais. Exposé au point de vue historique et militaire avec le concours d'un écrivain militaire distingué**, Berne, 1848. Accounts of the actions, large and small, organisation of the armies, tables of casualties, killed and wounded for both sides for each action of the war. Every casualty is named and with the nature of wound. A German-language edition (*Fraktur* script) was published in Zurich in 1848 with the title *Die neuesten Kriegsereignisse in der Schweiz, veranlasst durch die Berufung der Jesuiten nach Luzern und den im Bade Rothen gestifteten Sonderbund der Kantone Luzern, Uri, Schwyz, Unterwalden, Zug, Freiburg und Wallis; geschichtlich-militärisch dargestellt.*

Leuthy, Johann Jakob, *Die neuesten Kriegsereignisse in der Schweiz, veranlasst durch die Berufung der Jesuiten nach Luzern und den im Bade Rothen gestifteten Sonderbund der Kantone Luzern, Uri, Schwyz, Unterwalden, Zug, Freiburg und Wallis: Nachtrag** Zurich, 1849. Follow up to the above, contains further details of parts of the campaign and corrections to canton strengths.

Meyers, The Rev. M. J., *Note-Book of the late civil war in Switzerland. Chiefly for the use of travellers in that country**, London and Zurich 1848. A guide for English travellers in Switzerland with a description of the civil war.

Maillardoz, Francois Philippe de, *Mémoire sur ma participation aux événements de Fribourg en 1847**, Fribourg, 1850. A riposte by Maillardoz, who was accused of treason in surrendering Freiburg without a fight. Contains detailed organisation of the Freiburg army in the summer and autumn of 1847 besides a long defence of his actions.

Pacozzi, Renato, military specialist in canton Waadt (Vaud). Correspondence with the author.

Petitmermet, Roland & Rousselot, Lucien, *Schweizer Uniformen 1700-1850 = Uniformes suisses 1700-1850. Die Uniformen der Truppen der eidgenössischen Orte und Zugewandten von 1700 bis 1798 und der kantonalen Milizien von 1803 bis 1850,* Bern, 1976. A beautifully illustrated 'coffee table' book with 160 colour plates by Rousselot of groups of Swiss uniforms by canton and period. The text, in French and German, explains the plates and the artists' sources.

Remak, Joachim, *A Very Civil War: The Swiss Sonderbund War of 1847*, Boulder CO 1993. A well-researched book by a professor of history at the University of California. It is about the only modern book in English on the subject. Although published barely twenty years ago it is now increasingly difficult to find (ISBN 0-8133-1529-8).

Rudolf, J. M., *Die Geschichte der Ereignisse in der Schweiz seit der Aargauischen Klosteraufhebung 1841 bis zur Auflösung des Sonderbundes und der Ausweisung der Jesuiten; mit einer geschichtlichen Einleitung der Ereignisse von 1830 bis 1840, nebst Darstellung der Begebenheiten in Frankreich, Deutschland und Italien bis zum Juni 1848**, Zurich, 1848. In *Fraktur* script. Contains organisation and orders of battle in tabular format for Federal and Sonderbund cantons.

Rüstow, Wilhelm Friedrich, *L'art militaire au XIX siècle: stratégie, histoire militaire**, Paris 1869. Rüstow, a Prussian officer, was court-martialled for writing a 'liberal' tract and imprisoned. He escaped to Switzerland where he wrote on military history and in 1860 joined Garibaldi in Naples as his chief of staff.

Schneider, Hugo, *Vom Brustharnisch zum Waffenrock: das Wehrkleid des Schweizer Soldaten, 1650 bis 1915*, Frauenfeld, 1968. History of Swiss uniforms from 1650 to 1915. Includes also muskets, pistols, swords, headgear and equipment. Well illustrated with 80 plates, most in colour. Bilingual German and French text.

*Schweizerische Militär-Zeitschrift**, 1847. Appendices showing Swiss Confederation organisation and orders of battle as at the middle of November 1847 and the organisation of the Sonderbund forces. *Fraktur* script.

*Schweizerische Militär-Zeitschrift**, 1854. Includes an article about Swiss cavalry numbers in the 1847 campaign. *Fraktur* script.

Siegwart-Müller, Constantin, *Der Sieg der Gewalt über das Recht in der Schweizerischen Eidgenossenschaft,** Altdorf, 1866. A self-published book written nearly 20 years after the events by the former Sonderbund leader. Gives organisation of the Sonderbund armies and accounts of the battles from the Sonderbund point of view. *Fraktur* script.

Steinhäuslin, Charles Alexandre, *Bilder aus dem Sonderbundskriege im November 1847**, 1848. Steinhäuslin was already a talented artist before he joined the ranks of the Confederate army for the campaign, and recorded a number of characterful scenes of march and battle in pen and ink.

Zschokke, Heinrich & Zschokke, E., *The History of Switzerland for the Swiss People**, translated by Francis George Shaw, New York, 1855. A 'popular' history of Switzerland, written for an American audience, with the intention of making the European republic better known to the inhabitants of the sister republic in America.

various internet sites, search under 'Der Sonderbund'.

Index

BOOKS IN THIS SERIES:

1. *The Battle of Majuba Hill The Transvaal Campaign 1880–1881* John Laband (ISBN 978-1-911512-38-7)
2. *For Queen and Company Vignettes of the Irish Soldier in the Indian Mutiny* David Truesdale (ISBN 978-1-911512-79-0)
3. *The Furthest Garrison Imperial Regiments in New Zealand 1840–1870* Adam Davis (ISBN 978-1-911628-29-3)
4. *Victory Over Disease Resolving the Medical Crisis in the Crimean War, 1854–1856* Michael Hinton (ISBN 978-1-911628-31-6)
5. *Journey Through the Wilderness Garnet Wolseley's Canadian Red River Expedition of 1870* Paul McNicholls (ISBN 978-1-911628-30-9)
6. *Kitchener The Man Not The Myth* Anne Samson (ISBN 978-1-912866-45-8)
7. *The British and the Sikhs Discovery, Warfare and Friendship c1700–1900* Gurinder Singh Mann (ISBN 978-1-911628-24-8)
8. *Bazaine 1870 Scapegoat for a Nation* Quintin Barry (ISBN 978-1-913336-08-0)
9. *Redcoats in the Classroom The British Army's Schools For Soldiers and Their Children During the 19th Century* Howard R. Clarke (ISBN 978-1-912866-47-2)
10. *The Rescue They Called a Raid The Jameson Raid 1895–96* David Snape (ISBN 978-1-913118-77-8)
11. *Hungary 1848 The Winter Campaign* Christopher Pringle (ISBN 978-1-913118-78-5)
12. *The War of the Two Brothers The Portuguese Civil War 1828-1834* Sérgio Veludo Coelho (ISBN 978-1-914059-26-1)
14. *Forgotten Victorian Generals Studies in the Exercise of Command and Control in the British Army 1837–1901* Christopher Brice (editor) (ISBN 978-1-910777-20-6)
15. *The German War of 1866 The Bohemian and Moravian Campaign* Theodore Fontane (ISBN 978-1-914059-29-2)
16. *Dust of Glory The First Anglo-Afghan War 1839–1842, its Causes and Course* Bill Whitburn (ISBN 978-1-914059-33-9)
17. *Saarbruck to Sedan The Franco-German War 1870–1871 Volume 1* Ralph Weaver (ISBN 978-1-914059-88-9)
18. *The Battle of Lissa 1866 How the Industrial Revolution Changed the Face of Naval Warfare* Quintin Barry (ISBN 978-1-914059-92-6)
19. *The Zulu Kingdom and the Boer Invasion of 1837–1840* John Laband (ISBN 978-1-914059-89-6)
20. *The Fire of Venture Was in His Veins* Major Allan Wilson and the Shangani Patrol 1893 David Snape (ISBN 978-1-914059-90-2)
21. *From the Atacama to the Andes Battles of the War of the Pacific 1879–1883* Alan Curtis (ISBN 978-1-914059-90-2)
22. *The Rise of the Sikh Soldier The Sikh Warrior Through the Ages, c1700–1900* Gurinder Singh Mann (ISBN 978-1-915070-52-4)
23. *Victorian Crusaders British and Irish Volunteers in the Papal Army 1860–70* Nicholas Schofield (ISBN 978-1-915070-53-1)
24. *The Battle for the Swiepwald Austria's Fatal Blunder at Königgrätz, the climactic battle of the Austro-Prussian War, 3 July 1866* Ernst Heidrich (ISBN 978-1-915070-49-4)
25. *British Military Panoramas Battle in The Round, 1800–1914* Ian F.W. Beckett (ISBN 978-1-915113-84-9)
26. *Onwards to Omdurman The Anglo-Egyptian Campaign to Reconquer the Sudan, 1896–1898* Keith Surridge (ISBN 978-1-915070-51-7)
27. *Hungary 1849 The Summer Campaign* Wilhelm Ramming, Christopher Pringle (editor) (ISBN 978-1-915113-80-1)
28. *Line in the Sand French Foreign Legion Forts and Fortifications in Morocco 1900–1926* Richard Jeynes (ISBN 978-1-915113-83-2)
29. *The Republic Fights Back The Franco-German War 1870-1871 Volume 2* Ralph Weaver (ISBN 978-1-915070-50-0)
30. *Controlling the Frontier Southern Africa 1806–1828, The Cape Frontier Wars and The Fetcani Alarm* Hugh Driver (ISBN 978-1-915113-78-8)
31. *The Battle of Magersfontein Victory and defeat on the South African veld, 10–12 December 1899* Garth Benneyworth (ISBN 978-1-915113-79-5)
32. *Too Little Too Late The Campaign in West and South Germany June–July 1866* Michael Embree (ISBN 978-1-804513-77-4)
33. *The Destruction of the Imperial Army* Volume 1: The Opening Engagements of the Franco-German War 1870–71 Grenville Bird (ISBN 978-1-915113-81-8)
34. *Kitchener* The Man Not the Myth Anne Samson (ISBN 978-1-804513-84-2)
35. *From Ironclads to Dreadnoughts* The Development of the German Battleship, 1864–1918 Dirk Nottelmann & David M. Sullivan (ISBN 978-1-804511-84-8)
36. *The Destruction of the Imperial Army* Volume 2: The Battles around Metz Grenville Bird (ISBN 978-1-804511-85-5)
37. *More Work Than Glory* Buffalo Soldiers in the United States Army, 1866–1916 John P Langellier (ISBN 978-1-804513-34-7)
38. *The Spioenkop Campaign* The Battles to Relieve Ladysmith 17–27 January 1900 Robert Davidson (ISBN 978-1-804513-31-6)
39. *The Destruction of the Imperial Army* Volume 3: *The Sedan Campaign 1870* Grenville Bird (ISBN 978-1-804513-32-3)
40. *The Destruction of the Imperial Army* Volume 4: *Sedan, Strasbourg and Metz* 1870 Grenville Bird (ISBN 978-1-804514-59-7)
41. *Memorandum on the Prussian Army in Relation to the Campaign of 1866* Lieutenant Colonel W.E.M Reilly (ISBN 978-1-804516-27-0)
42. *Black Week: The British Army and Defeat in Anglo-Boer War 1899-1900* Quintin Barry (ISBN 978-1-804511 86-2)
43. *War in the East. A Military History of the Russo-Turkish War 1877-78* Quintin Barry (ISBN 978-1-804517-30-7)
44. *The First Schleswig-Holstein War 1848-50* Nick Svendsen (ISBN 978-1-804517-36-9)
45. *The Hundred Thousand Sons of St Louis* Ralph Weaver (ISBN 978-1-804517-37-6)
46. *Bismarck's First War: The Campaign in Schleswig and Jutland 1864* Michael Embree (ISBN 978-1-804517-38-3)
47. *The Honvéd War. Armies of the Hungarian War of Independence 1848-49* Nigel James Smith (ISBN 978-1-804514-60-3)
48. *Radestzky's Marches. The Campaigns of 1848 and 1849 in Upper Italy* Michael Embree (ISBN 978-1-804517-42-0)
49. *The Campaign on the Loire 1870-71: Orléans and Le Mans* Quintin Barry (ISBN 978-1-804517-82-6)
50. *The British Empire's Regulars 1880-1914: Soldiers of Britain, India and Africa* Wendell Scholander (ISBN 978-1-804515-62-4)
51. *The Last Throw of the Dice: Bourbaki and Werder in Eastern France 1870-71* Quintin Barry (ISBN 978-1-804517-78-9)
52. *Three Weeks in November. A Military History of the Swiss Civil War of 1847* Ralph Weaver (ISBN 978-1-804518-49-6)